Ritual
COMMUNICATION

To my first teachers,
Walter C. and Claribel W. Rothenbuhler

Ritual
COMMUNICATION

From
Everyday
Conversation
to
Mediated
Ceremony

Eric W. Rothenbuhler

SAGE Publications
International Educational and Professional Publisher
Thousand Oaks   London   New Delhi

For information:

SAGE Publications, Inc.
2455 Teller Road
Thousand Oaks, California 91320
E-mail: order@sagepub.com

SAGE Publications Ltd.
6 Bonhill Street
London EC2A 4PU
United Kingdom

SAGE Publications India Pvt. Ltd.
M-32 Market
Greater Kailash I
New Delhi 110 048 India

Printed in the United States of America

Library of Congress Cataloging-in-Publication Data

Rothenbuhler, Eric W.
Ritual communication: From everyday conversation to mediated ceremony / by Eric W. Rothenbuhler.
p. cm.
Includes bibliographical references (p.) and index. ISBN
0-7619-1586-9 (acid-free paper)
ISBN 0-7619-1587-7 (pbk.: acid-free paper)
1. Communication—Social aspects. 2. Ritual. 3. Social interaction. I. Title.
HM258 .R67 1998
302.2—ddc21   98-8971

This book is printed on acid-free paper.

98 99 00 01 02 03 10 9 8 7 6 5 4 3 2 1

Acquiring Editor:	Margaret H. Seawell
Editorial Assistant:	Renée Piernot
Production Editor:	Sanford Robinson
Editorial Assistant:	Nevair Kabakian
Designer/Typesetter:	Rebecca Evans
Cover Designer:	Candice Harman
Indexer:	Teri Greenberg

Contents

Part II
Ritual in Communication Research

Preface

Overview

This is a book on ritual, on the literature of ritual studies, on the use of the term *ritual* in the literature of communication studies, on ritual as a communicative phenomenon, and on communication as a ritual phenomenon. It is concerned with rituals as things, ritual ways of doing things, and ritual as a concept. It is a bibliographic essay, and an exercise in theory. Perhaps it has too many purposes in too few pages.

What do I mean by "ritual"? Obviously, ritual is a formal mode of action; obviously ritual emphasizes symbolic action over technically instrumental action; usually, ritual has something important to do with social relations and social orders. Eventually, by the end of Chapter 2, I will define ritual as the voluntary performance of appropriately patterned behavior to symbolically affect or participate in the serious life. I do not expect readers to understand the nuances and implications of that definition until after they have considered all the possible terms of definition found in the literature, as discussed in Chapters 2, 3, and 4. Besides, the word *ritual* has been used in many ways for many purposes, and one of the purposes of this book is to review those many uses. Were I to define ritual too narrowly or too soon, much of that review would be obviated. So the first half of the book has a predominantly inductive structure, based on the idea that we can learn much about the concept "ritual" by exploring the whole territory of its linguistic uses: What are the kinds of things in the world that are called ritual? What are the variety of things that scholars have had to say about ritual?

Chapters 2 through 5 are devoted to reviewing the literature of ritual studies, from anthropology and related fields (Grimes, 1987). This part of the book can be read as a bibliographic essay—I hope that readers will find it a useful guide to the literature. It is not just a literature review, though; I have a theoretical agenda and am evaluating the literature as I review it. I will have more to say about that agenda presently.

Chapter 6 is more explicitly devoted to original theoretical work than any other chapter in the book. In that chapter, I explicate a propositional argument leading to the conclusion that ritual is one of the strongest forms of communicative effectiveness we can identify, and show how its effectiveness works through its communicative devices. This theoretical work is necessary to receiving the full intellectual benefit of conceiving ritual as communication, and to the project of conceiving communication as ritual.

The second half of the book parallels the first. The first half begins by exploring definitions of ritual, works through the ritual studies literature, and concludes with a discussion of ritual as communication. The second half begins with the usefulness for communication studies of the idea of ritual, works through the communication studies literature, and concludes with a discussion of communication as ritual. Perhaps the two halves could be read independently of each other, or the second half as an application of ideas developed in the first. It is my hope, though, that the two halves will be read together, in the order they are presented, and that the book will be seen as a whole moving from the literature of ritual studies to the literature of communication studies, along the way identifing the roles communication scholars have to play in debates about the most general issues of social theory and social life.

The concluding chapter discusses a belief that motivated this work, a belief that I hope readers will see as justified by this work: that ritual is necessary to humane living together. There are a few presumptions to this. One is that order is necessary. So long as it is understood that by order I do not mean this or that political order, this or that historical circumstance, or this or that administrative arrangment, but rather that I mean order as a fundamental principle, as a basis of conscious experience and meaning, then that first presumption should not be controversial. Second, I presume that we cannot live apart, that we must live together. As a scientist, I am willing to consider the possibility of a disconfirming observation, but it is unlikely. As neither citizen nor scientist is that remote possibility my primary concern. We live together now, and that is what concerns me. Third, the historical record shows that it is possible for us to live together inhumanely, but that possibility is neither desirable nor inevitable.

If we must live together, then there must be mechanisms of coordination, particular orders must be made. Because ritual works by symbols, requires participation, and is open to reflection, it is a humane way of conducting social order. It is, then, necessary to humane living together.

Theoretical Agenda

Intellectual history is made of the struggle of schools of thought as much as the struggle with the facts. Concepts, logics, reasons, persuasion, tradition, and beauty play roles in scholarship that are not only independent of the facts but necessary to anything we might have that counts as knowledge of the facts. This makes our understanding of each other's ideas crucially important to any sensible growth of knowledge. Readers will be helped by knowing which intellectual traditions I am a part of and against which I am working.

This book is intended as a contribution to the tradition of debunking utilitarianism, to identifying the independent, arational roles played by symbols, meanings, and ideas. For present purposes, I locate the origin of that tradition with Émile Durkheim (1858-1917) whose first book, *The Division of Labor in Society* (1893/1984), was structured by the agenda of identifying the noncontractual element of contract, the moral basis of the economy, and the necessarily arational structures of supposedly rational modern societies.

Durkheim typically argued something like this: humans do not live by bread alone, by calculation alone, or as individuals alone, so biology, economics, and psychology are each incomplete in their account. What they each lack is attention to the independent role of social forces and structures in human life. We may calculate contracts, for example, but only in a society in which the idea of a contract already exists and is morally binding. Durkheim called his work the sociology of morals. Throughout his career, there was a shifting of emphasis that has led many to call his later work a moral sociology. This coincided with a radical growth in his attention to symbolic forms and processes as the devices for the social presence of that morality, so that his last book, *The Elementary Forms of the Religious Life* (1912/1965), can be read as positing a theory of the communicative foundations of social life.

My original interest in ritual began with *The Elementary Forms*. I hope that this book can carry that project forward. The book is structured to move the reader from an interest in the topic of ritual to the conclusion that ritual is a communication device necessary to humane society.

Debunking utilitarianism involves not only showing the limited role of instrumental calculation in everday life and the limited utility of utilitarian modes of explanation, it also involves arguing against some of utilitarianism's relatives: empiricism and materialism.

The history of science and ideas is clear that empiricism is wrong—not empirical work, without which there could be no science at all, but the particular philosophy of science called empiricism. Reasoning is a necessary independent component of all knowledge claims. It behooves us, then, to pay attention to it, to handle reasoning with as much discipline as we devote to methods of observation, to work as hard to make our reasoning intersubjective, as we do our data. This sensitivity to the independent role played by reasoning (and other ideas) in knowledge is parallel to, and anticipated by, the Durkheimian emphasis on the independent role of social forces represented in symbols and ideas. Just as society appears in the ideas and symbols it promulgates, so knowledge appears in the ideas and symbols of the social group that promulgates it.

Because of its antimaterialism, it is likely that this book will be seen by some as a statement of idealism. But adopting idealism does not necessarily follow from rejecting materialism. The goal is a synthetic theory, one that portrays a world in which the material and the ideal play independent parts, each in tension as they are pulled simultaneously by their own logics, constraining circumstances, and interrelations. This is the challenge of my teacher Jeffrey Alexander, especially as presented in the first volume of his *Theoretical Logic in Sociology* (1982).

Every instance of communication is obviously and necessarily a synthesis of the ideal and the material, the individual and the collective (Rothenbuhler, 1987; Shepherd & Rothenbuhler, 1991). For anything to count as communication, there must be about it some properties attributable to ideas (meanings, emotions, elements of internal experience) put in material form (written, spoken, recorded, externalized) by some individual (an action taken, by someone, for a purpose) in an order understandable by others (with a syntax, semantics, and pragmatics we can share, according to a sign system common to a group). From this simple understanding of communication as a synthesis of ideal and material, individual and collective, we can generalize to a synthetic social theory. Social life is a synthesis of ideal and material, individual and collective structures, forces, and processes. Antimaterialism in this case, then, is not based on idealism but is a response to the tendency of that school of thought to ignore, belittle, or even logically rule out the independent roles of the ideal and the individualistic in social life. (Admittedly, though, following from its topic, this book has its own idealist and collectivist biases.)

What the synthetic model, and attention to ritual, leads to is a vision of a world in which important aspects of social order are symbolically constructed and voluntarily enacted. That sentence is not as naive as it may appear. The nature of a historical era, the play of governments and corporations, and cultural currents are not dependent on individuals volunteering that they be so. The concern with ritual, though, draws attention to small everyday orders such as smiles and nods, offices with windows, and turn-taking in conversation, to recurrent ceremonies such as birthdays, reunions, Saturday nights out, and Sunday mornings at church. This level of everyday experience is where we find much of the social order of the world. Among family and friends, in the neighborhood and the workplace is where today is most like yesterday, this week like last, and where next year will be more or less like last year. In that order is not only repetition and boredom, not only social stratification and class, race, and sex-based exploitation, but also much that is meaningful, joyful, useful, and beautiful. Even that which is bad, or that may come in time to be seen as bad, can be more easily changed when it is an order that depends on ritual than when it is an order that depends on force.

Scholarship on social order is dominated by a vision of compulsion: power, force, law, violence, enforcement, punishment, exploitation are dominant terms. Order is conceived as based on discipline and enforcement, with the connotation of loss of freedom. Some analyses identify social order as repressed, and repressing, violence. But let us not lose track of the difference between physical violence that damages a living organism and metaphorical violence that requires wrestling with ideas. Mathematics, logic, painting, poetry, music, and preaching are disciplines, too. Discipline in this sense is something we take and something we do; it doesn't exist without us, and we engage it for its usefulness and its beauty.

I hope to rehabilitate ritual among those who treat it with suspicion. I want to point out its ubiquity and usefulness. I want to demonstrate its beauty and power. I want to point out that among the devices for order, it is one of the most gentle and most available to rational reform when it is needed.

Acknowledgments

My first thanks go to Steve Chaffee and Michael Schudson for inviting me to write on ritual as a communication concept, and providing encouragement and useful suggestions along the way. I also apologize to Steve and Michael for taking so long to finish the project. Thom McCain and Jane Frazer, co-directors of the Center for Advanced Study of Telecommunication at the Ohio State University, where I was Scholar-in-Residence January through March 1992, provided time for reading, thinking, and writing the first draft of a large part of this work. The faculty and students of the Department of Communication at Ohio State helped my thinking about the whole project. Bruce Gronbeck was instrumental in arranging my leave from Iowa for that period. The students in my seminars on ritual and communication at the University of Iowa and for one lovely summer at the University of Kansas were a special help in thinking through this material and helping me revise my thinking and expression. In addition to Chaffee and Schudson, Glenda Balas, Sam Becker, Kevin DeLuca, Steve Duck, Bruce Gronbeck, Elihu Katz, Hsin-I Liu, Donovan Ochs, John Peters, Chris Quinn, Michael Sáenz, Greg Shepherd, Sarah Stein, Doug Trank, Cathy Weingeist, and Barbie Zelizer have each read and commented helpfully on parts or versions of the manuscript. Jeff Alexander, Peter Clarke, Daniel Dayan, John Dimmick, Susan Evans, Elihu Katz, and the late Bill Hodge started me on this work. I hope they appreciate where it ended up.

Part I

What is Ritual?

Descriptions and Definitional Strategy

1.1

Social Life as Punctuated by Rites, Ceremonies, and Other Ritual Forms

A life is made up of birth, birthdays, comings of age, marriages, more births, acceptings, passings on, and death. Institutional life requires entering, passing through, and leaving; so we have initiations and welcomings, graduations and promotions, expulsions, resignations, firings, and retirements, dinners and parties and reunions. A work week is made up of beginning, middle, and end, a celebration, a rest, and then back to work again. A year is marked by New Year commemorations, celebrations of Spring, of mid-Summer, and of Autumn. Religious holidays are spread around the calendar by their communities, various minor holidays occur once a month or so, the birthdays of friends and family are personal holidays, a vacation, a convention, reunion, or family gathering or two, beginnings and endings of sports seasons all mark the calendar year. Special years also have the Olympics, national elections, and other political celebrations. These are all rites, ceremonies, conventions, and celebrations; both the progress and the cycle of time are marked by them. Some have elements of the spectacular and some are small, personal, and have no audience but the participants, some are more compulsory and some more voluntary, some extremely formal, some informal. These are all rituals and rituals are key features of the social life of every known society.

1.2

Ritual as a Symbolically Ordered
Component of Nearly All Social Action

Rites and ceremonies may have clearly delineated beginnings and endings that mark them as distinct events in the flow of social action, like religious ceremonies, for example. In addition there are ritualistic elements that appear within most social actions, as a feature of the action rather than an event separate from it. Thus ritual can be a way of doing things as well as a type of thing done; ritual can be a mode of social action, a feature, or stylistic aspect of social action. This is easily recognized in the formalized talk between superiors and subordinates in work organizations, but it also occurs between lovers, friends, and strangers. Indeed, in any social encounter there are markers of identity and intention that occur in a conventional form recognizable to strangers of the same culture. The smile and nod indicates friendly acknowledgement; the white uniform belongs to the nurse; a business suit facilitates the conduct of business; the person at "the head" of the table is in charge. These markers are articulated together across the flow of a single encounter and across the sequence of multiple encounters, so that aggregates of performances constitute recognizable characters, aggregates of similar performances by different people constitute recognizable roles, aggregates of different roles constitute recognizable social organizations, and so on. This systematic syntax constitutes a ritual order of interaction. This element of ritual appears in the trappings of office, tools and uniforms, personal style, deportment and demeanor, forms of talk—wherever form is emphasized in the symbolic elements we weave together in constructing a life.

1.3

Ritual as Noun and Adjective

The distinction between rituals as events and the ritual aspects of ongoing social activities will be important throughout this book. On the one hand are rituals, rites, and ceremonies as distinct events, types of activities, or social objects. On the other hand are the ritual or ceremonial aspects of otherwise ordinary and ongoing activities, processes, and events. In referring to the first case, we use *ritual* as a noun; in reference to the second, *ritual* becomes an adjective. More than one scholar has recommended against such potentially confusing multiple uses of the term (e.g., Grimes, 1990, pp. 9-15), but it is established in the language and the potential ambiguity is offset by useful flexibility.

The shift from ritual-noun to ritual-adjective not only allows a shift of referent—from rituals as things to ritual as an aspect of things—but of analytic point of view. It allows us to study communication *as* ritual as well as communication rituals. It allows us to study the ritual aspects of everyday television viewing as well as special media events. It allows us to study the ritual aspects of the everyday interpersonal communication through which relationships are conducted, as well as the ceremonial events that mark their major changes.

The apparent differences between the special event rituals and the ritual aspects of ordinary social activities can be large. Both, though, are elements of the moral regulation of social life. Both special ritual events and the ritual aspects of ordinary activities are part of the world of "oughts." In weddings and handshakes we promise to do what we ought. In funerals and saying goodbye we honor the other, promise to remember, and accept obligations to relationship. In everyday greetings we present ourselves as someone of definite character and promise to be that person, just as we expect presidents-elect to do in their inaugural ceremonies. The ritual aspects of ordinary social activities, then, are just as serious as the big, special event rituals. To anticipate the definition we will use later, they are both ways of using symbolic behavior to participate in the serious life.

1.4

Definitional Strategy

The territory of ritual studies encompasses otherwise diverse things such as handshakes and coronations, prayers, weddings, lovers' embraces, and vulgar gestures. Our concern encompasses formal rites large and small, celebrations, ceremonies, and spectacles. Of equal concern are the microsocial rituals of interpersonal deference and demeanor, presentations of self, the symbolics of authority, the trappings of office, and all the other ways in which "ritual is not a 'what,' not a 'thing' [but] a 'how,' a quality" (Grimes, 1990, p. 13).

Clearly, we face some definitional challenges. Ritual is a recognizable category, but it crosses and reorders myriad other categories of commonsense and social theory. Examples for ritual studies come from the realms of the religious and secular, archaic and modern, indigenous and colonial, political and personal, trivial and important, large and small, work and leisure, public and private, and from any cultural group available through the literatures of communication studies, anthropology, sociology, and historical, literary, and religious studies. Ritual, like other forms of communication, is everywhere.

A concept designed to cover a territory such as ritual is in danger of being vacuously abstract. Generalizing across such substantive diversity may leave nothing but a formal concept. In the case of ritual, though, it is precisely its formal qualities that distinguish it from other types of social action. Those formal qualities can be recognized in human action addressing a striking diversity of substantive meanings and purposes in a plethora of substantively diverse settings. Indeed, as we will see below, the form of ritual is a part of its meaning and necessary to its power. So it is to the form of ritual rather than its meanings, purposes, or circumstances that efforts at definition should be addressed.

Definitions

There are, in the literature of ritual studies, almost as many definitions as authors. Though there is no consensus on definition, there are some striking commonalities. There are also some contradictions. The place to start is with a review of the terms. Most of this chapter is devoted to discussion of 15 characteristics common to the many definitions of ritual available in the literature. (For different lists of terms and other useful discussions of definitions, see Gluckman, 1962; J. Goody, 1961; Grimes, 1990, pp. 9-15, 1995, pp. 58-74; Leach, 1968; Rappaport, 1979, pp. 173-221, 1989; Zuesse, 1987; see also J. Goody's, 1977, argument that the concept of ritual has become so all-inclusive and heterogenous as to be analytically worthless.) This review of terms ends with discussion of a communicative principle that is implicit in ritual and that has gone largely unnoticed in the literature (cf. Cheal, 1992). This communicative principle allows the integration of most of the key ideas from the other definitions reviewed into a single, formal definition of ritual. The chapter concludes with a discussion of that definition.

2.1

Common Terms of Definition

2.1.1 *Action*

Ritual is action, not just thought. That is sufficiently obvious for most authors today to take it for granted or allow it to be implied by other terms of their definition. In 19th century anthropology, though, the relation of myth and thought with ritual and action was a most important subject of debate, and Bell

(1992) demonstrates that it has structured much thinking about ritual ever since. Do myth and belief follow ritual action as an explanation or do they precede ritual action as a motivation? Tylor (1871/1924) and his followers saw myth as preceding ritual, so that activities would be classified as ritual because of the religious beliefs that accompanied them (whether this was simply a logical or also a historical precedence was another aspect of the argument). W. R. Smith (1889/1956) and his followers, of whom there were fewer, saw myth as follow-ing ritual—myth was the rationalization of the ritual activities. Such debates of precedence between action and thought are still very much with us, as in, for example, research on persuasion and the attitude-behavior relationship. In stud-ies of ritual, however, such otherwise hard dichotomies are often presented as if transcended; in ritual, many authors claim, belief and action become one, as the faithful in a religious service act out their faith, producing a world in which it is real (see Bell, 1992).

Another reason to emphasize the action/thinking dichotomy is that ethno-logical materials often provide evidence that the form of action in the rite is highly conservative, changing very slowly over succeeding generations, whereas the myths, beliefs, and explanations that accompany the rite are considerably more changeable, even appearing in different forms in the same community at the same time. The relationship between Catholic ritual and the beliefs of Catho-lics is one example; controversy over who should participate in St. Patrick's Day parades is another. The action of ritual and the thinking and feeling that accom-pany it can work in different ways with different results (Lincoln, 1989, provides comparative reviews of myth and ritual).

So the first point to make about ritual is that it is a form of action, not only a form or process of thinking. Ritual is something that people do bodily as well as thoughtfully, it has external form (Douglas, 1970/1982; Durkheim, 1912/1965). Second, though historical and comparative data show that external form may vary independently of the thought processes accompanying the ritual, for its participants, ritual often transcends that difference, producing an experiential unity of thought and action (Bell, 1992; Kertzer, 1988; Lincoln, 1989; Rappaport, 1979). As we will see below, that power of ritual is unique, and much of its effectiveness depends on it.

2.1.2 Performance

Ritual is performed, performance being "an aesthetically marked and height-ened mode of communication, framed in a special way and put on display for an audience" (Bauman, 1989, p. 262). In addition to the aesthetic emphasis (discussed below) the performative nature of ritual implies two interdependent characteristics. Ritual is a performance of something, for someone.

First, ritual is never invented in the moment of its action, it is always action according to pre-existing conceptions. These conceptions may be formally embodied, as in scripts for an actor or liturgies for a priest, or, at the other extreme, they may be present in latent competencies, such as those performed by a skillful host or an effective committee chair. At both extremes and all points in between, there are pre-existing conceptions that serve as both guide for the performance and criteria for its evaluation. (Note that the extent to which pre-existing conceptions are shared by the members of the scene in which a performance occurs is crucially important but is an independent question.)

Second, ritual is always performance for someone. Indeed, in the folklore and sociolinguistics literatures, this issue of being action for someone is often taken as the defining feature of performance: "Performance . . . consists in the assumption of responsibility to an audience for a display of communicative competence. . . . the act of expression on the part of the performer is thus marked as subject to evaluation for the way it is done" (Bauman, 1977, p. 11; see also, Abrahams, 1983; Bauman & Briggs, 1990). Not unlike nor unrelated to the continuum of pre-existing conceptions, running from latent competencies through formal scripts, the degree to which performance involves the acceptance of responsibility for the display of competence is also a continuum. This covers the range from simple "breakthroughs into performance" (Hymes, 1975), such as moments of showing off in the midst of otherwise ordinary conversation or instances of acting up in a committee meeting or classroom, through full-blown productions such as a symphony orchestra performance of standard repertoire, when everyone knows the score and the quality of performance counts as everything.

Important to all moments of performance, but easiest to identify toward the more formal end of the continuum, are the "keyings" of a frame (Goffman, 1974), within which the action is identified as performance of something for someone (Schechner, 1987). At the extreme of public ceremonial (e.g., B. Alexander, 1987; Dayan & Katz, 1992; Handelman, 1990) these keyings are ways in which a ceremony, such as a presidential inaugural, is set apart from ordinary affairs in terms of time, space, and modes of social action. Alteration of things such as word choice, tone of voice, style of dress, and rules of attendance are keys to the entrance and exit of a social frame. Such keys are reflexive symbols that both mark a boundary in social action and offer information about the other action within that boundary.

When the issue of displaying competence is taken as primary, the categories of ritual performance and artistic performance can merge. The cantor and the opera tenor can both be judged by the beauty of their singing, irrespective of the divergent natures of their texts, settings, and audiences. This may be appropriate for performance studies, but students of ritual will need to distinguish ritual from art and entertainment. The display of competence, then, though important, cannot be taken as the primary issue of ritual performance. Having said that, however, it should not be forgotten that ritual and art have been importantly interdependent throughout human history (Harrison, 1913), and though ritual may be a special type of performance, not identifiable with all displays of competence, to the extent the effectiveness of ritual depends on the form of its performance, the competence of that performance will be crucial.

2.1.3 *Conscious, Voluntary*

There is always something conscious and therefore voluntary about ritual. In the case of special event rituals, people are aware that they are participating in them, that they are performers or witnesses, and usually that the occurrence of the ritual is not something naturally or physically necessary but a human accomplishment. In the case of smaller, less especially distinct rituals such as interpersonal displays, people are often not fully conscious of their behavior nor do they experience any real effort. Handshakes are easy and often thoughtlessly, even if not insincerely, given. Nevertheless, people always can be, and often are, aware of choices embedded in ritual interaction forms. Depending on the ritual, of course, they might choose to participate or not, choose the mode of their participation (e.g., performer or witness), choose the orthodoxy of their performance, choose the style and enthusiasm of their participation, and so on.

This issue of choice, and the necessity that actors invest their energy in a ritual in order that it be performed, means that the performance of a ritual, and hence any results, are contingent on its actors. Ritual has this in common with any other sort of human action. This formal voluntarism, J. C. Alexander (1978, 1982) argues convincingly, is a feature of all human action, while the issue of substantive voluntarism—what in the right circumstances we might call freedom—remains a separate question. In the unique case of ritual action, however, the formal voluntarism has substantive implications.

Almost always, rituals are accompanied by a certain social compulsion. The costs that result from choosing not to participate may be such that we do not experience certain rituals as voluntary. Refusing to swear allegiance to the king can be costly, but swearing allegiance is only valid for those who utter the words themselves and if it is indeed possible that they not do so. In such circumstances, volitions are a necessary component of the action; hence, the action is formally voluntaristic. Formal voluntarism has a substantive implication in cases such as this, because of the meaning of the ritual. The ritual participant accepts, rather than resists, the social compulsion; he or she performs that acceptance in the ritual (cf. Rappaport, 1979, pp. 173-221).

2.1.4. *Noninstrumental or Irrational*

Many authors address instrumentality, rationality, or the nature of means-ends relations in their definitions of ritual by classifying ritual as noninstrumental, arational, or irrational action (e.g., Gluckman, 1962; J. Goody, 1961; Parsons, 1944/1954). The same idea appears in analysis of politeness as a deviation from "the rational and efficient nature of talk" (Brown & Levinson, 1987, p. 4) and in assigning the label ritual to television viewing that is not instrumentally motivated by information-seeking goals (e.g., Rubin, 1984).

Ritual is called arational or nonrational to the extent that it is not useful for specifically technical purposes. The standards of scientific or technical rationality do not apply to it because the means-ends relations are not intrinsic from the point of view of the scientific observer (see Parsons, 1937/1968). Rituals used for technical purposes or in some other way treated as if they were instrumental, then, would be labeled magic, or it would be said that the ritual or its use is irrational. This follows Frazer's famous 19th century definition of magic as "the bastard science" because it uses "expressive acts which purport to alter the state of the world by metaphysical means" instead of "technical acts which alter the state of the world by physical means" (quoted in Leach, 1976, p. 29). More recent but still classic discussions are offered by Malinowski (1922/1953, 1948) and Weber (1922/1978, pp. 422-442).

Obviously it is not true that all rituals are noninstrumental in all ways, even though noninstrumentality has been a dominant theme in the literature. Even if technical rituals such as magic or divination cannot be shown to causally bring about their desired ends, they can be shown to perform other social functions that are just as practical, such as reducing indecision, producing consensus, and inspiring groups to action (e.g., Wallace, 1966, pp. 171-173). If the magic associated with canoe building and sailing among the Trobriand Islanders helped them to coordinate their actions and allowed them to sail with confidence and thus to succeed in the face of danger and uncertainty, this practical result should be a focus of the analysis of ritual (Malinowski, 1922/1953). In modern societies, many ceremonial behaviors can be shown to serve similarly practical social functions. Wallace (1966, p. 236) includes the functions of reduction of anxiety, preparation for action, and social coordination in his definition of ritual. Ritual might not be the only means, or technically the most efficient means to an end, but it can get certain jobs done. In addition, many historical rituals appear to have functioned as devices for memory, socialization, or other forms of storing social knowledge. The repetition characteristic of ritual may not be rationally connected to the purported purpose of the ritual, but it is a rational approach to producing memory or reinforcing social roles and relations. Certainly ritual forms such as commemorations, visits to monuments, and repeated story telling—as at Passover and Easter—are essential to collective memory (Halbwachs, 1992; Zerubavel, 1995).

Finally, the point of identifying the so-called arational element of ritual is that ritual works by a logic of signs, meanings, and morals that is distinct from the logic of technical rationality (see Lévi-Strauss, 1958/1963, pp. 167-205 on ritual; Parsons, 1937/1968; Weber, 1922/1978, pp. 3-307, on different forms of rationality for different types of action). If a handshake cements a deal, it may be a very practical affair performed instrumentally but it does not work through a medium of causality, it works morally (see Durkheim, 1893/1984, pp. 317-320, 1958/1983 on the moral basis of contract; Bateson, 1972/1987, pp. xxiii-xxvi, 432-473; Rappaport, 1979, pp. 97-144 on the different logics of systems of energy and systems of meaning).

2.1.5 Not Recreational

Rituals are not just recreational. There is often celebration associated with ritual, but rituals are not only for fun. Even the fun and frivolity have serious functions: funerals end with meals, political conventions include balloons and silly hats, carnival leads to Lent, bachelor parties put a close on an era of life. Though its gratifications may be important, the meaning of a ritual is not exhausted by them. In short, ritual is part of the serious life (Durkheim, 1912/1965, e.g., pp. 424 ff.; Pickering, 1984, pp. 352-361; Shils, 1975, esp. pp. 153-163).

This idea of the serious life deserves more discussion. It originates in Durkheim's writing as "la vie sérieuse," and was, for him, the positive pole of a dichotomy with the not-serious, the carefree, or recreational. Durkheim's most productive use of the distinction was in analysis of religious ceremonies, arguing that some of the activities had a serious object and hence were ritually necessary, whereas others arose from spontaneous expression, aesthetics, convenience, or habit. This allowed him to avoid the pitfalls of assuming that everything has a necessary social function. Elsewhere in Durkheim's writings, though, the not-serious is a residual category holding everything he valued less than the most earnest concentration of attention on scientifically defined reality (e.g., 1925/1973, pp. 267-281). Everything from leisure activities and diversions to the greatest artistic productions was lumped together and disparaged as not part of the serious life.

Rather than following Durkheim strictly, it is better to follow Pickering's (1984, pp. 358-361) advice and use the serious life as an ideal type rather than as defining a dichotomy. It is also useful to follow Shils's (1975) example and use serious as an emic term, for a kind of phenomenological analysis. In this way, the serious life labels an attitude of the people we study rather than an observer's evaluation of their activities. These important ideas will be elaborated as they recur in the discussion and are used in analyses (sections 2.1.12 & 2.1.15; Chapters 8 & 11). For present definitional purposes, it will do to state that "ritual in contrast [to play], is in earnest, even when it is playful, entertaining, blasphemous, humorous, or ludicrous" (Rappaport, 1979, p. 177). (See also MacAloon, 1984; Turner, 1982a, 1982b, for studies of the serious functions of ritual frivolity.)

2.1.6 *Collective, Social*

By most definitions, ritual is not something individuals do only for individual purpose in purely individualistic ways. Rituals can, of course, be performed in private, but there is always something socially structured about them: language and other sign systems, tradition, systems of morality. Some women refer to their daily routines of facial and body preparation and caretaking as beauty rituals. To the extent that word use is apt (see cautions about equating ritual and routine in sec. 3.1), it is because these are repetitive and collectively structured actions that embody cultural codes, even though they are done individually and in private. Even in Freud's conception of individual ritualistic behavior (critiqued in sec. 4.2) it is identified as a symptom of a pathology with origins in social relations. Usually, rituals are oriented toward a group and most often performed in social situations. As J. Goody (1961, p. 146) points out, "the two meanings of convention, an assembly and a custom, are not accidental." Not only are rituals performed in social situations and structured by social phenomena, they also have social meanings. They refer to relationship and social position (Leach, 1968); they are a way of indicating and embarking on socially oriented intentions (Goffman, 1959, 1967).

2.1.7 *Expressive of Social Relations*

Ritual "involves the use of modes of behavior which are expressive of social relationships" (Gluckman, 1962, p. 22). The forms of ritual action constitute symbols that often have among their referents the social relations, orders, and institutions of the society in which the ritual is performed. So for example, the slight tipping of the head and downward glance of the eyes that subordinates will perform when shaking the hand of a superior is a ritual enactment of the superior-subordinate relationship. Similarly, the vestments of the various ranks of the Catholic Church indicate positions of power within the institution, as well as closeness to God. The rituals and other symbolic activities with which all societies surround sexual differences, relations, and reproduction, render biological phenomena as matters of social relations (Lutkehaus & Roscoe, 1995; K. E. Paige & J. M. Paige, 1981).

Generations of British structural-functionalists took the claim that ritual expresses social relations as axiomatic and used its presumed truth as a methodological device. The idea was that from a reading of the ritual of a society, one could map its social structure (see Radcliffe-Brown, 1952/1965; Bloch, 1989, is insightfully critical of this method). Leach's later work (e.g., 1976) constructs a new rationale for the same basic idea, based on linguistic structuralism and the French, rather than the British, anthropological tradition. The same idea, but taken as a research problem rather than an axiom, is what motivated Goffman's work on interaction rituals, in which "the divisions and hierarchies of social structure are depicted microecologically" (1976, p. 1, see also 1959, 1967). Burke advances a similar strategy, as is especially clear in *The Rhetoric of Religion* (1961/1970, see also 1966, 1973, 1989). He finds structures of language, structures of meaning, and structures of social life all in correspondence. His model of language as symbolic action breaks down the commonsense distinctions among these orders, rendering the relationships magically transformative (cf. Leach, 1976, pp. 37-41, on ritual condensation).

To speak is to perform language: language is not meaning, but its performance both expresses and produces meaning. So meaning both precedes language use and follows it. Meaning, then, both produces and is created by language just as language both produces and is created by meaning. To speak is to embody language and meaning, which is to place both in a position in a social order; to embody language and meaning in a position in a social order is to perform a position in a social order, which is to constitute it. So the social order both gives rise to language and meaning and is a result of language and meaning.

In this system of relations, one form is always becoming the other, and that mode of becoming is a kind of ritual transformation.

Even short of that elaborate structure, no one doubts that some significant part of what rituals are is a symbolic expression of the social orders in which they are found (cf. Leach, 1968). These orders may range from the relatively informal relations of the performers to the whole structure of institutional powers.

2.1.8 *Subjunctive, Not Indicative*

Rituals often occur in the subjunctive mood. They are often not about what is, but what could be, might be, or ought to be. Initiations and inaugurals, for example, usually require humility of the ruler-to-be, who swears to be a servant of the people, claims to be unworthy of the task, and so on (Turner, 1969/1977). Political ceremonies and conventions usually celebrate values and beliefs to which few maintain fidelity outside the ceremony (MacAloon, 1982). Religious ceremonies require behavior expressive of attitudes and ideas—supplication or awe, for example—widely recognized as inappropriate outside the ceremony. Civic commemorations of cultural heroes promote near impossible standards of propriety.

Turner (1969/1977, 1975, 1982b) and his school (e.g., MacAloon, 1984b; Moore & Myerhoff, 1975; 1977; Turner, 1982a) have explored the relation between ritual and ordinary social life in detail. That relationship is one of reflection, commentary, evaluation, and hope. As Handelman (1990) discusses, rituals may operate as models of a version of social order, they may present an idea of social order, or they may re-present ideas of social order, but they never simply reflect a structural status quo.

Many critics of ritual make the mistake of expecting rites and ceremonies to be indicative. Judged that way, many of them are obviously false—they do not accurately describe the world in which they occur. But viewed as time-outs from the usual constraints of practical affairs, they are occasions for imagining how things could be or evaluating how they ought to be. This is an important social function, not to be minimized.

There is another facet to the subjunctive mood of ritual. As Gennep (1908/1960) identified and Turner (1969/1977; 1982b) later analyzed, the structure of many rituals includes a liminal space, a threshold or in-between place or time. This constitutes a time-out from normal social roles, responsibilities, rules, orders, and even modes of thought. A religious service is a time-out from the work world, during which banker and borrower, corporate vice president and loading dock worker participate as equals. A wedding day is a time-out from ordinary days that falls between the status of being single and the socially more freighted status of being married.

These liminal periods can produce a great degree of license in social activity and a potential for freedom and creativity in social thought. Carnival, conventions, football games, and bachelor parties all show degrees of licentious behavior that is, to varying degrees, ritually prescribed (e.g., Turner, 1982a). One is supposed to sin during carnival, just as delegates are supposed to wear silly hats at political conventions. Certain artistic and intellectual scenes and famous moments in history have also been liminal to their surroundings, this being ritually marked and characterized by unusual freedom of activity and creativity of thought: Weimar Germany, Paris in the 1920s, the Summer of Love, May 1968, and Prague in 1992, for example.

2.1.9 Effective Symbols

The symbols of a ritual are seriously effective. Above and beyond the ordinary ways that language use gets things done, the symbols of ritual are powerful. The power of ritual symbols is clearest in rites of passage and other transformational rituals (e.g., Gennep, 1908/1960; Myerhoff, Camino, & Turner, 1987) in which boys turn into men, girls into women, single individuals into married couples, the citizens of one country into the citizens of another, private citizens into public servants or soldiers and back again. Equivalently powerful symbols are at work in all ritual, even when social transformations are not the explicit purpose of the ritual, as song, dance, gesture, prayer, communion, sacrifice, costumes, masks, architecture, and so on alter psychic and social experience (e.g., Bloch, 1989, pp. 19-45; Goodman, 1988; Turner, 1967, 1982a; Young-Laughlin & Laughlin, 1988). This effectivity of symbols is a fundamentally important point that we will discuss at greater length in Chapter 6 (see Austin, 1962/1975, and Lévi-Strauss, 1958/1963, pp. 167-205, for foundational arguments).

2.1.10 Condensed Symbols

Ever since Geertz's (1973) essays on "thick description" and the Balinese cockfight became paradigms for cultural analysis, it has been implicitly understood that socially important symbols have layers of meaning and multiple, simultaneous referents. Thus social analysts must unpack the meanings, examine the laminations, and follow the ramifications, for the full meaning of socially important symbols is not clear from their surface. One of the reasons is that most socially important symbols are characterized by condensation, a term used in slightly different forms in anthropology and psychology.

Sapir (1934/1949) distinguished referential from condensation symbolism, the latter characterized by multiple referents, richness of meaning, "a highly condensed form of substitutive behavior for direct expression, allowing for the ready release of emotional tension" (p. 565), with "deeper roots in the unconscious and diffus[ing] its emotional quality to types of behavior or situations apparently far removed from the original meaning of the symbol" (p. 566).

For Freud (1913/1937, pp. 269-272), condensation was an aspect of the dream-work, the process of transformation by which unconscious thoughts became dream-content. One of the features of the relationship between dream-content and dream-thoughts is that dream-content is highly condensed. This condensation is evident in at least three ways: the volume of dream-content is much smaller than that of dream-thoughts; each element of dream-content will be found to have multiple determinants in dream-thought; and most important, the most vivid and intense elements of a dream are those that have been subjected to the greatest degree of condensation, those with the largest number of determinants in dream-thought (p. 315). The result is that "the intensity of an entire train of thought may ultimately be concentrated in a single conceptual unit. . . . ideas which are of great psychic significance as nodal points or as end-results of whole chains of thought" can come to be represented in the intensity of some wholly other idea, represented in the dream (p. 547).

In more recent anthropological usage, condensation refers to the characteristic of ritual symbols that multiple meanings, actions, and things may be represented at once. For example, Turner (1967) says "the milk tree stands for, *inter alia,* women's breasts, motherhood, a novice at *Nkang'a,* the principle of matriliny, a specific matrilineage, learning, and the unity and persistence of Ndembu society" (p. 28). Aside from the need to account for all these meanings, the emphasis is on the functions and implications of condensation itself and the particular cluster of meanings condensed in a given ritual symbol (see Turner's, 1978, account of the influence of Freud's *Interpretation of Dreams* on his own work; cf. Leach, 1976, pp. 37-41, for a technically distinct usage).

For the religious—and that includes those under the sway of patriotism or nationalism—condensed symbols explode with meaning when released in the ritual situation. Ordinary objects like flags, uniforms, crosses, and vestments expand to fill their situations with meaning. They flood consciousness, reducing the significance of ego as it is washed over by what is experienced as the inevitable flow of meaning. In Turner's (1967) analysis, the condensed nature of ritual symbols allows their emotional and ideological meanings to become fused in the ceremony and its aftermaths.

> In the action situation of ritual, with its social excitement and directly physi-ological stimuli, such as music, singing, dancing, alcohol, incense, and bizarre modes of dress, the ritual symbol, we may perhaps say, effects an interchange of qualities. . . . The irksomeness of moral constraint is transformed into the "love of virtue." (p. 30)

Such condensed symbols are also richly ambiguous—not only difficult for the social observer, they are extraordinarily flexible, adaptable to multiple social uses. Such symbols can work in different ways for different people simultane-ously, depending on their sensitivity to different valences. The effectivity of such symbols can carry over from one situation to another. The emotional valences attached to symbols in one situation can be ritually called up in another, and some of the power of that emotion can be used to other ends. This appears commonly in the use of national symbols and appeals to patriotism in non-national contexts such as schools, ballgames, and partisan politics. Condensation is key to the political uses of ritual (Kertzer, 1988).

There is another implication of condensation. From the point of view of the participant, the condensed nature of the symbols of ritual means that they are supersaturated. These are symbols that hold more meaning than is normally possible; they may, thus, begin to precipitate into multivocality at the slightest jar—just as a supersaturated liquid will give up a solid precipitate and a liquid remainder the instant a too-careless stirring scratches a crystal into formation. In the right circumstances a handshake has positive social effects on a number of levels simultaneously. However, when we begin to think about it, its meaning can quickly fall apart, as we try to trace out the referents: A friendly gesture, a sign of no-threat, a cementing of brotherhood, a reinactment of parent-child relations, a rule taught for getting ahead in business, an ancient manly rite, a silly anachronism? The working of condensation depends on faith, lack of attention, or misdirection of attention, and it does not hold up well under cynical exami-nation. Because of its capacity to unpack the condensed symbols of ritual, ex-posing the sometimes dubious referents, critical reflection can be hostile to rit-ual, as Grimes (1990) discusses at greater length. Similarly, as Sapir (1934/1949) pointed out, when social change removes the normalized pattern of behavior that supported a condensed symbol, it can suddenly appear to be unmasked, having little or no referent or function.

The need for a certain "unthinkingness" for the effectiveness of ritual symbols—usually through condensation of multiple referents and valences—is identified as its insidiousness by some (e.g., Bloch, 1989) and its transcendence by others (e.g., Rappaport, 1979). This argument is a recurrent theme throughout this book, and aspects of it are addressed in sections 3.5, 5.2, and 6.5, as well as in the concluding chapter. Here it will suffice to conclude with Turner's (1967) acknowledgment that

> ritual symbol has, in common with the dream symbol, the characteristic, discovered by Freud, of being a compromise formation between two main opposing tendencies. It is a compromise between the need for social control, and certain innate and universal human drives whose complete gratification would result in a breakdown of that control. (p. 37)

The implications of adopting this position are that the evaluation of the ritual must depend, in part, on the nature of the compromise and the qualities of the resulting order; the results can be healthy or pathological (cf. Bateson, 1972/1987, p. 473).

2.1.11 *Expressive or Aesthetic Behavior, Aesthetic Excess*

Many definitions of ritual emphasize the expressive or aesthetic element; Leach's (1968) famous definition of ritual as the expressive aspect of behavior depends crucially on it. Others take stylistic, symbolic, or aesthetic excess to be a marker of ritual. Defining ritual by reference to aesthetic excess will be critiqued in section 3.4, but using aesthetic excess as a methodological device to identify ritual is a common strategy that deserves separate discussion. If something is stylized beyond reason, the aesthetic is emphasized in an otherwise practical realm, or symbolism is emphasized as a stylistic device, then that is taken to indicate the presence of ritual attitudes. For example, entering a room can be seen as a goal-directed activity; doing so to the accompaniment of a band playing "Hail to the Chief" as uniformed guards snap to attention and all in the audience rise to their feet can be seen as an activity marked by aesthetic excess and hence, ritualized.

The logic of defining ritual as aesthetic behavior depends on distinguishing practical from expressive acts, identifying the former with utility and materiality, and the latter with aesthetics, symbols, and ideas. This appeals to common sense and can be useful, yet Sahlins (1976, pp. 166-204) shows that the distinction of practical from expressive is itself a symbolic construction, expressive of ideas, and eminently aesthetic.

> The reason Americans deem dogs inedible and cattle "food" is no more percep-
> tible to the senses than is the price of meat. Likewise, what stamps trousers
> masculine and skirts as feminine has no necessary connection with their physical
> properties or the relations arising therefrom. It is [rather] by their correlations
> in a symbolic system . . . (Sahlins, 1976, pp. 169-170)

He goes on to show that the symbolic relations of cows and pigs, horses and dogs, and nearness to domestic space in American culture define the desirability, or taboo, of the various animals as food. He provides a yet more elaborate analysis of the materials, colors, patterns, and construction techniques of different clothing for different genders, classes, and cultural expressions. The analyses implicitly depend on identifying the symbolic or expressive aspect of things by comparison to a standard of material necessity or utility, essentially following the logic that defines ritual as arational or irrational (see secs. 2.1.4 and 3.4). He then demonstrates that utility, if not also materiality, is itself a cultural category, defined in a system of symbols.

This points to one of the difficulties of style and aesthetics as terms of definition for ritual. Taken alone, style, symbols, expression, and aesthetics imply too broad a definition of ritual. Aligned with the notion of excess, they require some standard of judgment. That inevitably turns out to be technical rationality, utilitarianism, or some other such scheme essentially unsympathetic to ritual phenomena (Douglas, 1970/1982) or simply naive as to its own cultural foundations (Sahlins, 1976).

But something important is being identified here. The expressive *is* one of the key modes of ritual; it is part of what rituals do and part of how they do it. Rituals also have an essential aesthetic component; many of them are aesthetically fabulous. But even the more humble are more aesthetic than technically practical, more symbolically expressive than physically causal.

2.1.12 *Customary Behavior*

Rituals are forms of customary behavior. This is key; no definition of ritual is adequate without it. There is always something about ritual that is stereotyped, standardized, stylized, relatively invariant, formal. This implies that ritual is repetitive in the sense that others have done it this way before. This also implies again the earlier point that ritual is not authored by the actor; it is, to at least some degree, a performance of a script.

It must, however, be clear: Behavior is not customary just because it is regular, uniform, or constant. That is an element, but what is essential for customary behavior is that it is behavior according to custom, that is, according to a rule or standard. Customs are external standards for judging behavior. Customary behavior, then, is an imperative, ethical, and social order. The imperative may be large or small, the ethic most serious or mostly optional—remember, we are trying to encompass handshakes, coronations, and religious services—but this is a region of behavior governed by oughts. There are right and wrong ways to do things; choices in this realm have implications that are serious (see secs. 2.1.5 & 2.1.15).

2.1.13 *Regularly Recurring Behavior*

Ritual is also repetitive in another sense. In addition to being behavior that has been done this way before by others, ritual is regularly recurring. Many rituals are calendrical, being prescribed by the repetition of a cycle rather than the mere passage of time. Even those rituals that mark the passage of time from the individual's point of view, such as rites of transition from one social age to another, still are regularly recurring in the social aggregate. Ritual performance has its own social rhythm.

One of the important implications of the cyclical appearance of rituals is that they are not dictated by situation-specific things, but by verities. This is true by definition of calendrical rites, but is only true—in a certain way, from a certain point of view—of others. Take the rite of passage from one social age-grade to another (Gennep, 1908/1960). That would appear to be dictated by a situation-specific phenomenon: when people get to a certain biological age, the rite is engaged to move them to the next social age. But it is not substantively dictated by situation-specific things; bar mitzvahs, baptisms, debutante balls, and other transitions through puberty or to the initiation of adult responsibilities (18th or 21st birthdays, for example) happen when they are dictated by the norms of social groups, not when the individuals involved are necessarily ready for them. In many Mexican American communities the 15th birthday is a rite of passage from girl to young woman, regardless of the specific maturity of the young person in question.

A more complex example is provided by the ritual cycle presented by Rappaport (1968) in *Pigs for the Ancestors.* As Rappaport demonstrates, the cycle of ceremonies of the Tsembaga in New Guinea is tied to various ecological cycles such as the pig population, the age and fertility of garden plots, and the calories expended on gardening and other labor. The cycles operate together as a cybernetic system, the whole being adapted to relevant ecological processes. The ritual cycle is also substantively tied to treaties, alliances, fighting, courting, marriages, and trade with neighboring groups. Yet the meaning of each rite as well as the whole cycle is cast in religious terms, in reference to the sacred, the ancestors, and moral principles. So the individual ritual performances are as deeply embedded in their situation as any ritual could be, they also succeed each other in a cycle that, once initiated, proceeds by its own logic, not by reference to ecological or social particulars, and the whole is woven into a meaningful pattern made up of the basic verities of social life.

2.1.14 *Communication Without Information*

Some authors have pointed out that ritual is communication without information, or at least that ritual is communication that works in peculiar ways from the point of view of information theory (Bloch, 1989; Rappaport, 1979; Wallace, 1966).

In information theory, the statistical problem of predicting message content—for example, what will the next word be? what will the next letter be?—is used to generate a numerical measure of information as the degree of choice in composing messages (Shannon & Weaver, 1949/1963). Note that this is quite distinct from the meaning of a message. When this logic is turned on ritual, it is noted that rituals are stereotyped, characterized by liturgy, repetition, and an emphasis on form over substance, and thus do not offer many choices of message composition. Therefore, it is said, they do not carry much, if any, information in that statistical sense. It is also pointed out that rituals are loosely tied to the specifics of the situation in which they occur—their timing dependent on calendar rather than event, for example—and therefore they are not informative about those specifics.

These are important observations, but the claim that ritual is communication without information can easily be overstated. If it is true that there is something voluntary about ritual, then the act of participation reflects a choice and thus contains a bit of information. The timing of ritual, too, is always informative in some way. Even calendrical cycles are informing in the way that they are mapped onto the passage of time in experience.

At any rate, the idea that ritual is communication without information points to something important: ritual has more to do with performing than with informing, more to do with transcendent patterns of order than with particularities, sometimes more to do with acceptance than with change. (See Rappaport, 1979, pp. 173-246, for careful delineation of the different types of sign in ritual and their varying capacities to inform, perform, give meaning, and so on.)

2.1.15 *Regarding the Sacred, an Element of the Serious Life*

Finally, many authors emphasize that ritual is action regarding the sacred. This *is* the definition for Durkheim (1912/1965, e.g., pp. 51-57). It is a key part of any definition in the Durkheimian tradition and many others also emphasize it (e.g., Eliade, 1959; Eliade & Sullivan, 1987; Zuesse, 1987). Others argue explicitly *contra* the Durkheimian tradition—that the sacred is a flawed and unhelpful concept.

The concept of the sacred has intuitive appeal for students of religious ritual. The problem is that the substance of the sacred varies wildly from community to community, culture to culture, historical setting to historical setting. This creates difficulties in categorizing social activities, objects, and ideas as sacred or profane. Body movements that may be sacred for a yogi, would be profane for a protestant. Musical instruments and styles of singing encouraged as worship in the Church of God in Christ are prohibited as sinful in the Church of Christ.

Substantively delineating sacred and profane realms, activities, and things is very difficult, often unreliable. Lutgendorf (1990a), for example, discusses historical shifts and contemporary controversies in the definition and use of sacred words and stories in North India, pointing out that "sociopolitical as well as religiocultural" (p. 115) factors are at work. When the *Ramayana* became the basis for a television serial—which became one of the most popular weekly shows on television in India, not only generating large commercial revenues and pirate videos but inspiring devotional activities centered on television watching, which in turn was criticized by the cosmopolitan press—obviously the distinction of sacred and profane in that setting had only grown more complex (Lutgendorf, 1990b).

Despite these difficulties, many scholars recognize structural similarities across human cultures and situations in action toward the sacred (e.g., Eliade, 1952/1991; Eliade & Sullivan, 1987; Zuesse, 1987). A formal definition of the sacred identifies those commonalities and avoids any statement on the variable particulars. In any given cultural community, the sacred is whatever is treated as unquestionable, "beyond interdiction" as Durkheim puts it, as of the utmost seriousness by the members of that community. (Obviously, this depends on a definition of group that includes some consensus of opinion—a theoretical strategy that has been widely criticized as unrealistic to the plurality and diversity of modern social structures—but functional consensus need not be unrealistically defined as unanimity of group opinion (Shils, 1975, pp. 164-181). Also obviously, observers' judgments of what is treated as unquestionably serious must be comparative and relative.)

The criterion of sacredness is the pattern of activity of the members of the community, how they treat a sacred object—such as the grape juice used in a Protestant communion, for example—rather than the object's nature independent of their treatment. Such patterns of activity, reflecting a tendency to treat some things as of a different category of importance, appear to be a constant of human social life. At a formal level, as Durkheim (1912/1965) first pointed out, that is the foundation of religious thinking: not gods or spirits or myth, but the fact that every human group treats some things as unquestionably serious.

> As long as the category of the 'serious' remains in human life, there will be a profound impulse to acknowledge and express the appreciation of that 'seriousness' in words and actions of symbolic import. (Shils, 1966, p. 449)

When the sacred is defined by reference to human activity rather than divinity, ultimate power, or some other transcendence, it is taken to be a matter of human experience, the experience of seriousness. "The serious life" is the phrase coined by Durkheim to identify those features of the social world united in their attention to such things (picking up our discussion from sec. 2.1.5).

The serious life is a phenomenological category, its boundaries and substance shifting with the human experience of which it is a part. Formally, it is that enduring and ubiquitous recognition that some things are more important than others, and that some ideas, symbols, and activities are so important that they deserve to be set aside and protected (Douglas, 1966/1978; Durkheim, 1912/1965; Shils, 1975, esp. pp. 111-235). Religious practices, as Durkheim (1912/1965) analyzed them, put the faithful in contact with the sacred while preventing inappropriate mixing of sacred and profane. A church, its architecture and furnishings, special times for attendance, special clothes and manners of conduct, the activities that begin, conduct, and conclude a service, are all rituals of approach and avoidance that allow controlled contact with the sacred forces of a community. These same structures can be observed in nationalist and patriotic ceremonies. Generalizing from this model, ritual events allow celebrants to participate in the serious life, however they may define it. This functional definition of religion is eminently generalizable, and has allowed Durkheimian analyses to be used profitably throughout the fields of cultural studies (e.g., J. C. Alexander, 1988b).

Does this same dimension appear in the ritual aspects of everyday life? Yes, though clearly in attenuated and structurally different form. The handshake, the promise, and the civil presentation of self are features of the moral regulation of everyday life. Because they are part of the routine, we do not usually experience them as special, or as especially serious. But when a promise is broken, when a presentation of self turns out to have been dishonest, or when the competence or emotional control necessary for civil performance is lacking, the sense of violation is palpable. In such circumstances, things are out of order and it is not order alone that is at risk (Douglas, 1966/1978). Socially, our ritually structured conduct of ourselves, on examination, turns out to be who we are (Goffman, 1959, 1967). Even if it can usually be handled relatively thoughtlessly, there could be no more serious matter.

Ritual, then, in all its forms, is an element of the serious life. Sometimes ritual events are explicitly addressed to the sacred as recognized by their participants. Sometimes ritual events are addressed to serious issues that the participants identify as secular—political, economic, family—but which scholars can recognize as structurally identical with the referents of the faithful in religious ceremony. In another form, the ritual elements of everyday life are often thoughtlessly, though not insincerely, performed—it is only on analysis that they can also be seen to be elements of the serious life, ritual mechanisms for the moral regulation of secular affairs.

2.2

A Communicative Principle and a Final Definition

In concluding the discussion of terms and logics of definitions of ritual, we will push through to a couple of fundamentals, including a communicative principle that is characteristic of *all* human ritual. The discussion will conclude with a formal definition of ritual that explicitly states or logically implies each of the essential terms of the preceding discussion, leaving the other terms as descriptive of common characteristics of ritual, but not formally necessary.

One fundamental might be called the seed of ritual, or less metaphorically, its generative logic. Wherever ritual appears, appropriately patterned behavior constitutes symbols that are effective beyond the behavior itself. Without this generative logic, nothing could be a ritual; all rituals presuppose it (Leach, 1968).

Notice how many of the key ideas from the previous discussion of terms of definition are either present in or implied by the statement "appropriately patterned behavior constitutes symbols that are effective beyond the behavior itself." The stipulation that the behavior be *patterned* addresses the stereotypy and formality of rituals—though questions of the degree and nature of patterning remain. That the behavior be *appropriately* patterned implies the existence of rules and the performance of a script not authored by the actor. Further, the reference to appropriateness implies external support for the behavior—in the case of ritual, an institution, moral system, sacred presence, or cosmic structure. The symbolic element is explicit, as is its material basis in human behavior; the ideal reference is implied by the term symbol. The effectivity of the symbols is explicit. The fact that the effectivity is "beyond the behavior itself" identifies the nonintrinsic means-ends relation.

Notice that this generative logic of ritual—that appropriately patterned behavior constitutes symbols that are effective beyond the behavior itself—must also be the generative logic of communication. No act of communication could be such unless that logic held; all acts of communication presuppose it. Ritual and communication are kin; they are logically related and share family characteristics (Cheal, 1992; Leach, 1968, 1976). There has already been occasion to comment on the communicative aspects of ritual. Chapter 6 addresses the more formal, logical relations of communication and ritual, working with a conception of ritual as communication. Part 2 of the book reviews conceptions of ritual in communication studies, concluding with a discussion of communication *as* ritual.

All such discussions depend on the almost always unidentified presupposition of a communicative principle: Everyone who performs a ritual accepts the idea, at least implicitly, that his or her patterned behavior is symbolically meaningful and effective. That is, participants in ritual are doing something symbolically; they are using symbols to achieve social purposes.

This communicative principle implies one more of the essential terms from the discussion of definitions, voluntarism, though such a vexed issue should not be allowed to be only implicit. One remaining key term is not implied by the communicative principle, reference to the serious life. Adding those two terms, then, produces this formal definition of ritual:

> *Ritual is the voluntary performance of appropriately patterned behavior to symbolically effect or participate in the serious life.*

This is a maximally general, formally rigorous, yet substantively flexible definition. If carefully used, such a definition should capture the whole range of rituals from handshakes to coronations in the whole range of human societies, while clearly distinguishing between ritual and related communication forms. Admittedly, though, the rules for distinguishing between ritual and other communication forms depend on elaborations and explications that are not present in the definition itself but worked out in the rest of the book.

Five Inadequate Conceptions

Habit and Routine

One common use of the word *ritual* is to designate a habit or routine. For example, some people say they have a morning ritual or that watching the news every evening is a ritual. The word *ritual* is being used here essentially as a synonym for habit or routine and those words capture the phenomenon well enough. Sometimes the word ritual is used for very important habits or routines, but then adjectives can be used to get the point across.

If a conception of ritual is founded on the definition of ritual as habitual or routine action, then we have serious problems. Such a conception is completely inadequate to the social importance, meaningfulness, and effectivity of common rituals such as weddings, funerals, baptisms, oaths, initiations, and even every-day politeness. Habits lack what energizes rituals: the purpose of symbolically effecting the serious life.

Habits are, as well, prevalent features of social life and communication. The problems of confusing ritual and habit can be made more clear with examples from the communication studies literature.

Gerbner and his colleagues (e.g., Gerbner & Gross, 1976; Gerbner, Gross, Morgan, & Signorielli, 1986) claim that much television viewing is by the clock and the calendar, that audiences are largely not selective of programs and watch instead by habit. They say such media use is ritualistic. A contrast is often drawn with the view of the audience as active, hence purposeful, as assumed by the uses and gratifications school (e.g., Katz, Blumler, & Gurevitch, 1974). Ritual- ized television viewing, conceived in this way, is a kind of thoughtless viewing, governed by habit. Examination, though, shows that this is an incoherent con- cept, defined by contrast with instrumentality, and thus nothing really but a re- sidual category (see sec. 8.2 for a different definition of ritualized media use).

Rubin's (1984) "ritualized and instrumental television viewing" is the most well known examination of this conception of ritualized television viewing and also has the benefit of being carefully data-based—we can thus examine both conceptual and operational definitions.

"Instrumental media use [is defined as] goal-directed use of media content to gratify informational needs or motives and ritualized media use [is defined as] more or less habitualized use of a medium to gratify diversionary needs or motives" (1984, p. 69). The patterns of correlations in Rubin's data show "mo- tivations usually associated with ritualized television use [include] escape, habit, arousal, passing time, and relaxation" (p. 71);

> evidence of ritualized television use . . . includes positive relationships among the motives of using TV for companionship, out of habit, to pass the time, for economic reasons, and for entertainment, relaxation, and arousal. Associated with this type of viewing were action/adventure, game, music/variety, drama, and general comedy programs. (p. 73)

In short, "ritualized" television use is anything other than purposefully seeking a specific type of information and is associated with watching anything other than news and information programming. It is a residual category and there is little positive sense to be made of a concept that might be both relaxation and arousal, entertainment and habit, companionship and economy.

The key point of Rubin's (1984) study, though, is not a concept of ritual but that the "activity" of the audience member comes in a variety of forms and is exhibited in degrees. This is an important point for communication theory, not to be dismissed by criticism here of the use of the word *ritual.* It would also be counterproductive to draw researchers' attention away from the importance of habitual behavior. It is undoubtedly true that a large proportion of communica- tive acts are thoughtlessly performed; certainly much media use is structured by habit. Habits provide much of the stable order of the social world and are useful tools for allocating cognitive resources and for efficiently adapting to situations (see Camic, 1986, for a thorough review). This being said, a habit is not a ritual, nor is it even ritual-like.

3.2

Insincere Public Performance

It is also inadequate to conceive of ritual as insincere public performance. Often enough public officials, bureaucrats, public relations agents, and others act as if they are genuinely motivated by honest concern for the issues at hand when in fact they are not. When politicians and media personalities profess concern about "the drug war," prefer telegenic events to difficult policy decisions, and say nothing about the alcoholic beverage business or its advertising and campaign contributions on which they depend, their actions could be called ritual rather than real. When employees know that company management is not proud of them and does not want their participation in any thoughtful way, then an employee award ceremony could be labelled "just a ritual."

Here is an example from the communication studies literature:

> Science or ritual dance? [Rowland] sees television violence research as a ritual dance in which academics were led by politicians looking for juicy issues, by industry looking for a safe legislative dead end, and by reformers looking for experts to support their claims and their illusions. The ritual fooled no one but the public. (Gerbner, 1984, p. 164)

In this example, the action of studying television violence is seen as not being genuinely related to people's motivations. The claim is that no one really wanted to do anything about television violence; rather, they wanted to gain publicity, research grants, or distraction.

The heterogeneity of these examples is a clue that this is another instance of defining ritual as a residual category. Here, rather than being noninstrumental, ritual is not-genuine or not-real. Misappropriation of the term *ritual* to identify insincere public performances results in two serious problems for ritual studies scholars. First, it undermines the ability to distinguish ritual from insincere public behavior, because it assumes that the two are synonymous.

Second, the presumption that ritual is display unconnected to underlying realities becomes a habit of thought that MacAloon (1982) usefully calls the complex of the mere-'s. Once we begin to think in this way, mere-ritual, mere-ceremony, mere-spectacle, mere-rhetoric, mere-symbol, et cetera are seen as equally unworthy of respect or attention. All symbolic forms become distrusted; they appear to be not fundamentally real but only second-class realities in need of some other form of assurance (Peters & Rothenbuhler, 1989). Obviously this presumption is untrue to both academic pursuits and everyday realities—spoken with passion, "I love you" or "Go fuck yourself" could never be taken as mere-performance meaning nothing. What's more, such thinking is logically danger-ous, for a model social world built on these principles would have no base other than that which could be assured by Newtonian physics; it would be a world ruled by brute physicality (Rothenbuhler, 1988b).

3.3

Empty Convention

A use of the term *ritual* closely related to habit and not unlike insincere public performance is in regard to empty conventions. Almost everyone has had the experience of going through the motions of something that is supposed to be a meaningful ritual but is not. It has the form but not the substance of ritual. Company picnics for which attendance is mandatory, reunions among people who don't really care, church attendance for those with no faith are all examples of empty conventions. When people are just going through the motions, they will often say it is "just a ritual" (e.g., Haines, 1988). These are roughly equiva-lent to social habits, things a group does because they have always done so and not because the activities are particularly meaningful in themselves and in this moment. Like insincere public performances, these activities are not strongly motivated by their apparent meaning. The participants do not really care about the events as much as their participation appears to indicate, but unlike insincere public performances, an empty convention is just empty, we usually do not sus-pect its participants of bad intent.

Empty conventions are real enough phenomena and a theory of ritual needs to be able to address them, but building a conception of ritual on such examples is a flawed strategy. In doing so, the pathological is treated as the normal, and the ability to understand rituals that work is lost. Haines (1988) documents the ambivalent uses of the word *ritual* in family communication, sometimes to in-dicate something important and sometimes to indicate something that has lost its importance. His work shows that we must distinguish these uses of the term *ritual* in order to analyze the ways it can go wrong.

The case of politeness shows how complex the issues are. Being polite to people we dislike is commonly given as an example of empty convention. In some ways, it may be that insincere politeness is a pathological ritual; in other ways, it is not. Politeness, whether it is motivated by caring for others or not, is one of the most important and powerful rituals of social order. In being polite, we perform civil society. In performing civil society, we create it. At that point, in some ways, it no longer matters what we think of the person with whom we are being polite, our relations with them will be civil nevertheless—and that may be the main point of this particular ritual.

3.4

Stylistic, Symbolic, or Aesthetic Excess

Another conception of ritual that falls short of our theoretical needs is ritual as stylistic, symbolic, or aesthetic excess. This definition comes into play when it is necessary to distinguish the ritualistic features of an activity or artifact. The phenomenon is analyzed as a means to an end and the features not necessary to that relation are defined as excess. If the excess follows stylistic, symbolic, or aesthetic conventions that are associated with social relations, it may be identified as a ritual element of the action or artifact. Information theory (Shannon & Weaver, 1949/1963) can be used in the same way. The signs of a text or performance are evaluated for the unique and necessary information they carry. Redundant signs and those unnecessary to the message are categorized as elements of style (Milic, 1987). For example, one way or another it is necessary to say "hello" in order to greet someone. However, if one does so floridly rather than simply and according to social conventions, those elements defined as unnecessary can be seen as ritual. To say "Hi, Charlie" is one thing, to say "Good morning, Dean Jones, and how are you today? Is there anything I can get for you?" is another. The latter, by this definition, would be seen as embodying a ritual display of respect, along with greeting. That it does. But to identify all rituals according to excess entails at least two serious problems. First it fails to identify the ritual element of social actions that are not aesthetically excessive; second, it isolates ritual and labels it excessive, hence unnecessary.

Defining ritual as symbolic excess does draw attention to important features of ritual. *How* things are said and done is as important in ritual as *what* is said and done. Rituals work through symbols that do not necessarily have intrinsic means-ends relations (according to the criterion of instrumental rationality). Many rituals are characterized by a great redundancy of symbols, stylistic elaborations, and an emphasis on aesthetic criteria that can well seem excessive.

But not all rituals have a thickness of symbols. The simple "Hi, Charlie" can, in the right context, in a history of relation, with the right body movements and vocal inflections, be a symbolic performance of informality, personal comfort, or even intimacy. As interpersonal communication researchers have established, all communication has a layer that defines relation even as something else entirely is being said (Watzlawick, Beavin, & Jackson, 1967). Some define this ritual *as* ritual—the aspects of communication that are expressive of social relations—but this does not in any way depend on a criterion of excess. There is an element of the expression of social relations in the simplest of communication acts.

In addition, any definition of ritual that depends on a criterion such as excess sets up dichotomies that remove ritual from the world of the practical, real, rational, or simple and then implicitly denigrates it as impractical, unreal, irrational, and overwrought. As noted, this makes it difficult to understand how ritual can ever be used to get anything done. Further, such a criterion prefers a plain, brutal world. When aesthetics are evaluated by reference to the instrumentality of means-ends relations or the efficient delivery of information, nonaesthetic criteria and a logic that is fundamentally anti-aesthetic are used. In a world that values only efficiency, nothing but efficiency would be beautiful.

The bottom line is that ritual cannot be understood without attention to style, symbol, and aesthetics—they are essential to its work. For the same reason, ritual cannot be understood if its stylistic, symbolic, and aesthetic elements are defined as excessive.

3.5

Ritual = Myth = Ideology = Lying or Confusion

Barthes (1957/1972) carried a classic mode of Marxist analysis over into cultural criticism. As the ruling ideas are presumed to be the ideas of the ruling class, the ideas encoded in the most popular cultural forms must be those that support, while hiding, the interests of the ruling class. The critic's job, then, is to unmask the class interests lying behind popular culture and to teach the masses to see through the trick of popularity. When this form of analysis is applied to ritual, the performance of ritual is seen as akin to the promulgation of myth, which, if not presented as class interest, is a form of lying or of confusion. So much is often true.

The empirical prevalence of a set of associations, however, should not be confused with the logical association of a set of analytical terms (Barthes, 1957/1972, pp. 145-149, distinguishes these but blurs them in much of the rest of the book—and certainly the influence of the book is not based on this careful distinction but on the heroic unmasking). The results would put conclusions before analysis, take hypotheses as facts. The implicit logic of most applications of Barthes's myth analysis is: if this is myth it must be conservative; if this is a bourgeois society, conservation is bad.

Such simplistic thinking was already criticized by Trotsky (1924/1960) as intrinsically unable to handle the complexity of cultural phenomena (Deutscher, 1959, pp. 164-200). Trotsky (1973) also understood that rituals, ceremonies, myths, and icons were important features of the complex textures of everyday life. If the revolution was to succeed it could not simply banish the rituals of the prior society, it must replace them with new ones. The new rituals must be built on the values of the revolution but function as well as the old for the meaningful integration of everyday life. Gramsci's writings on popular culture in the *Prison Notebooks* (1971) can also be read, in part, as addressing much the same ideas.

Ideology is an essential issue in social research, and the tradition of Marxist theory has been a major source of insight into its workings. Rituals attract the critical attention of Marxist thinkers because of their prevalent association with central institutions and ideas, and thus their close association with power. They often do ideological work, and this must be analyzed. But neither our understanding of ritual nor of ideology is promoted by facile critiques that replace analysis with debunking, questions with presumptions, agnosticism with hostility. The social orders we are trying to understand are complicated; so must be our explanations of them.

The main point is that every social order must have symbolic means of maintenance and adaptation. Myth and ritual will be among those. If we are to critique ritual, it must be a substantive critique, based on the values and beliefs that are being promulgated and not a formal critique, based simply on the fact that it is a ritual. In complex societies, rituals and their uses and results are complex; so must be our analyses of them (Lincoln, 1989). Our work of interpretation is a "hermeneutics [that] must combine the attitude of trust with an attitude of suspicion" (Kohák, 1966, p. xxxi).

In addition to these substantive concerns, there is also the problem that the idea that ritual = myth = ideology = lying or confusion works by assuming that the participants and audiences of myth and ritual are confused. Some people some of the time certainly are, but that empirical observation is not a logical principle on which to build a theory. It leaves us completely unable to explain why some people are *not* confused and, more important, unable to account for the meaningful experiences that people have via ritual and myth.

Two other points: Note that equating ritual with lying or confusion, like other definitions I have criticized, removes ritual and constrains it to the world of the unreal or the distrusted (see MacAloon, 1982, 1984a; Peters & Rothenbuhler, 1989; Rothenbuhler, 1988b). Second, as we will see in more detail below, this definition simply cannot deal with the ubiquity of rituals and the variety of their results.

4

Four Only Partly
Adequate Conceptions

4.1

Ethological

For the ethologist, the student of animal behavior, a ritual is a conspicuous, patterned behavior with signalling function. Rituals are displays, the result of an evolutionary process of ritualization by which normally motivated behaviors have been formalized or canalized "(a) to promote better and more unambiguous signal function, both intra- and inter-specifically; (b) to serve as more efficient stimulators or releasers of more efficient patterns of action in other individuals; (c) to reduce intra-specific damage; and (d) to serve as sexual or social bonding mechanisms" (Huxley, 1966a, p. 250; see also, Eibl-Eibesfeldt, 1975; Etkin, 1967; Hinde, 1982; Huxley, 1966b; Lorenz, 1970-71; W. J. Smith, 1977; and Tinbergen, 1972-73).

The gist of the ethologists' concern is behaviors that have communicative function—which they call ritual behaviors—and the process by which they develop—called ritualization. We recognize the function of feeding behavior and the stimuli that trigger it, but what are the functions and causes of displays such as head tossing and facing away in gulls (Tinbergen, 1972-73, pp. 44-46)? The dominant explanation, as built into Huxley's definition of ritualization, is that such displays are behaviors with greater than normal conspicuousness and stereotypy, and therefore less than normal ambiguity as a signal. Such displays are adaptive at the species level and thus a product of evolutionary selection:

> Whenever it is of advantage for an animal that some of its incidental behavior be understood by another, selection operates to transform the behavior pattern in question into a conspicuous signal. . . . [, a] modification of a behavior pattern to serve communicative function. (Eibl-Eibesfeldt, 1975, p. 110)

There are important lessons in the ethological literature for the student of human communication, but the differences between the two fields are great and complex. A very few authors have made important contributions to communication theory and ritual studies by explicitly working to encompass animal behavior and evolutionary principles—notably, Bateson (1972/1987) and Rappaport (1979)—but they are also extraordinarily careful about the differences between human society and animal biology, between the human and the biological sciences.

The question of subjective experience is methodologically ruled out in ethology (e.g., Lorenz, 1970-71; Tinbergen, 1972-73), but it is the foundation of the human sciences (Dilthey, 1989) and essential to any adequate social theory (Parsons, 1937/1968; Schutz, 1932/1967; Weber, 1922/1978). As the ethologists themselves point out (e.g., Tinbergen, 1972-73, Vol. 2, pp. 202-203), culture far dominates genetic evolution both in the timespan of human history and in the current social situation. For the ethologist, communication is essentially limited to signalling and its "meaning" is identified with resulting behavioral changes (e.g., W. J. Smith, 1977). Such a conception is completely inadequate for the study of human communication and culture.

There are yet more differences at the level of specific propositions about ritual. Leach (1966) puts the issues forcefully: The definition of ritualization used by the ethologists

> has no relevance for the work of social anthropologists. . . . For the ethologist, ritual is adaptive repetitive behaviour which is characteristic of a whole species; for the anthropologist, ritual is occasional behaviour by particular members of a single culture. This contrast is very radical. . . . It cannot be too strongly emphasized that ritual, in the anthropologist's sense, is in no way whatsoever a genetic endowment of the species. . . . From the ethologist's point of view an example of ritualized adaptation in *Homo sapiens* is the capacity for speech, but the evolutionary developments which resulted in this capacity took place a very long time ago and the findings of contemporary anthropology have absolutely no bearing on the matter. (p. 403)

Because the ethologists are working at a different structural level than those of us in the human sciences (evolutionary time and specieswide phenomena vs.

historical time and cultural and individual variance) the phenomena they identify as human ritual are just the starting points for our analyses. To point out that speaking behavior is an evolutionary adaptation does not even provide clues as to the questions that constitute the substantive study of human communication. Gombrich (1966) points out that human communicative forms take on a range that is collapsed in animal behavior; the friendship ritual *is* friendship for the goose (at least, so far as we know), but it is only part of the experience for humans. Corresponding to the greater range of representative forms that our outward movements can make and their potential alienation from our inward experience is the whole problem of their adequacy: "I suspect that animals are rarely plagued by this feeling of inadequacy when they perform a ritualized act of submission or ingratiation. For animals probably lack that distinctively human achievement, the lie" (Gombrich, 1966, p. 398; see also Bateson, 1972/1987, on deceit and on "not," another phenomenon characteristic of human experience to which other animals show no sensitivity).

But as the work of Bateson (1972/1987) and Rappaport (1979), among others, makes clear, there are things for the student of human communication and culture to learn from careful reading of the ethological literature. Of course, humans do have an evolutionary history and a physiological basis; of course, human communication is also a pattern of behavior. The strict comparative behavioral method of the ethologists can help identify the basic mechanisms of ritual communication, its mechanical, behavioral, and formal substrates, and their powerful evolutionary theory draws attention to the most general constants of communication in human social life (see esp. Rappaport, 1979, pp. 145-172, 223-246).

As an example of the behavioral contribution, here is Eibl-Eibesfeldt's (1975) list of changes that may occur in a behavior during a process of ritualization:

1. The behavior undergoes a change of function. The original food enticing . . . [for example, becomes] a courtship behavior. . . .
2. The ritualized movement can become independent from its original motivation and develop its own motivating mechanisms. . . .
3. The movements are frequently exaggerated in respect to frequency and amplitude, but they are at the same time simplified, by the dropping out of some components while others become exaggerated. . . .
4. The threshold values for releasing stimuli often change to such a degree that the more ritualized behavior pattern, in general, is more easily released. . . .
5. Movements frequently "freeze" into postures. . . .
6. Components of orientation are changed. . . .

7. A behavior pattern that had previously varied in response to the intensity of motivation and stimulus can become stereotyped, with constant intensity. . . .
8. Variable movement sequences can become compressed into stereotyped and simpler ones. . . .
9. Along with these behavioral changes there frequently occurs the development of very conspicuous body structures, such as ornamental plumes, enlarged claws for waving, manes, sailfins, and tumescent bodies. (pp. 113-114, emphasis deleted)

If, instead of food enticing and enlarged claws, the examples were subordination, stiff postures, and colorful robes, this list could have been addressed to human ritual behavior. (Of course, the reason ritual animal behavior looks like ritual human behavior is not only because of evolutionary continuities but because the ethologists borrowed the term *ritual* from the humanities, to describe animal behavior that reminded them of humans.) Though the ethologists would have nothing to say of the meaning or experience of ritual, or any effects other than the behavioral, as observers of behavior, they are superb.

As Goffman (1976) points out, there is also something to learn from the ethologists' general orientation. For the ethologists, ritual behavior is communicative behavior. Hence, it always has a significance in a situation involving other animals; it is oriented to that situation, those others, and an unfolding course of behavior. The ethologists identify the aspect of ritual that is future and other oriented. The animal engaged in display is making information available about its current alignment in the situation and its likely course of action. Among the animals exhibiting rudimentary social behavior, this includes signs complex enough to offer information about the significance with which the behavior about to be performed should be taken: attack, play, courtship, defense, indifference, and so on. This is obvious. But studies of human ritual usually emphasize an orientation toward the cosmic or mysterious, the mythic past or tradition, sometimes to the relative exclusion of the usefulness of ritual in the current and unfolding social situation (some functionalist theories, though, counterbalance this, e.g., Wallace, 1966). The emphasis on communication in the ethological study of ritual is a useful complement to the usual emphases of ritual studies in the humanities literatures.

Even this contribution must be taken in context. It would be of no benefit to communication studies to follow the ethologists' example so far that ritual behavior became equated with communication behavior. We already possess a far more elaborated conceptual apparatus. Our interest in ritual is as a type of communication and as an aspect of communication. Humans have many ways to communicate their orientations and intentions. Collective ritual events are one way that groups can do it; the ceremonial aspects of interpersonal interactions are one way that individuals can do it. The ethologists remind us that these are useful activities with a future orientation. We must remind the ethologists, though, that for their human participants these are activities of great seriousness, referring to ideas as well as behaviors.

4.2

Freudian

Freud wrote influentially on ritual and religion, culture and society. This work both assumed and set out to demonstrate a significant analogy between ritual and symptomatic obsessive behavior and, therefore, also between religion and neurosis (see Freud, 1913/1950, 1921/1959, 1928/1961, 1930/1961, 1939/1964). It is controversial whether he should be read as offering expert analysis of an isomorphism, as using metaphors to generate insight into some small, previously dark corner of religious phenomena, or as engaging in rhetorical flourish (Gay, 1979). There is the small yet powerful claim that ritual acts have something structural in common with obsessive behavior, and the much larger but also weaker claim that religion is like neurosis. At any rate, the ideas are connected to a prevalent lay use of the word *ritual* to refer to symptomatic patterns of small, repeated behaviors that may make the actor feel safer but that do not "actually" do anything. Acts such as frequent hand washing, or wiping one's feet every time one passes through a door are behavioral quirks that appear to be more connected to a psychological preference for cleanliness than to the physical presence of dirt.

Without the symptomatology, the Freudian view of ritual—and the related lay use—degenerate into the definition of ritual as habitual behavior that we have already rejected. With the symptomatology, it puts the student of ritual in a disadvantageous position. From the start, analysts must assume there is something pathological about ritual action. As that is not how most ritualants experience their action, analysts are in no position to understand or explain the meaning of the ritual in a manner adequate to the participants' own subjective orientations. (Freud's psychoanalysis had the advantage that it was ordinarily applied to patients who knew that something about their thought processes was peculiar and, through the long communicative process of psychoanalysis, he brought them to an understanding that was adequate both to their original experience and to scientific understanding.)

But there are some useful points in the Freudian analysis. The first contribution of the Freudian analysis of ritual is the key insight that the ritual action is a sign of something not otherwise physically present, something phenomenologically elsewhere and elsewhen. Freud's analysis of the non-psychopathological is marked by an identification of symbols and symptoms inherent to the simultaneous concern with explanation and treatment (Ricoeur, 1981, pp. 254-264). When recast in neutral terms of signs and signifier-signified relations, the Freudian analysis of ritual behavior draws attention to one of its key features: that the behavior is a sign of something else, something it is not.

Second, it is important that the meanings of ritualized signifier-signified relations may go deeper than the present awareness of the actors, even as it is the basis for the power of their experience. This is a key issue for Ricoeur's (1970, 1974, pp. 99-208) phenomenological philosophy; the point can also be made on a less fundamental level. There is, in important rituals, something numinous, something mysteriously self-powering that gives the experience a force for the faithful beyond their ability to recast the meaning in words (Zuesse, 1987). In Sapir's (1934/1949) formulation of condensation symbols, an important feature was their "deep roots" in unconscious or only marginally conscious thought; the different referents condensed in a ritual symbol were connected, for the most part, unconsciously. Ritual symbols work on consciousness by a logic that is mostly not in consciousness.

4.3

Sentiment and Solidarity

The most familiar part of Durkheim's social theory is the function of ritual in maintaining the social order, specifically by way of sentiment and solidarity (Durkheim, 1912/1965). Holidays and holy days require a break in the normal social routine. That time is usually used for reunion and reflection. People gather together and spend time thinking about their relations and about ideals and moral principles—about the way their world ought to be. By periodically requiring a time-out, assembling the disparate social members, and engaging in a celebration of the affective bonds and moral principles they share, ritual functions to reinvigorate the social order. All involved return to their daily rounds, strengthened and refreshed, reminded of their social role, the rules of their social order, and their dependencies on one another. This part of Durkheim's writing is easy to caricature but it also provides a key insight into how society—in part—works. It has inspired many followers (e.g., Dayan & Katz, 1988, 1992; Geertz, 1977; Rothenbuhler, 1988c, 1989, 1995; Schramm, 1965; Shils & Young, 1956/1975; Warner, 1959).

This part of Durkheim's work is important; but alone it is too simple a theory, in two related ways. First, it overemphasizes the maintenance of a given social order—an issue addressed in the next section. Second, it posits a too simple idea of the devices of social order: that society is held together mostly by sentiments, solidarity, and consensus. The functions of ritual would be, then, to reinforce our agreement, our positive feelings for each other, and our bonding with the whole society. Though such ideas do help to explain the effects of certain processes and events in which sentiment and solidarity are emphasized—such as the American public's response to the assassination and broadcast funeral of President Kennedy (Greenberg & Parker, 1965)—such ideas are too simple to explain the whole workings of a complex society, or any ritual for which multiple interpretations are prevalent. Thus, overdependence on sentiment as an explanatory concept is a weakness in Kertzer's (1988) otherwise excellent treatment of ritual in modern social life and political processes.

As Lukes (1972, 1975) points out, this part of the neo-Durkheimian tradition has made the mistake of shearing Durkheim of his cognitive element. The roles of ritual and religion in promulgating basic beliefs as well as moral principles and affective ties were important to Durkheim's theory. More fundamentally, Durkheim recognized (though he did not theorize it well) that religion and ritual participated in the construction of basic cognitive categories and logics (see 1912/1965, e.g., pp. 21-33; Durkheim & Mauss, 1903/1963). Hence, ritual and religion give shape to the stuff of which even profane thought and action are constructed. As rituals promulgate definitions of reality, forms of thought, and modes of evaluation, they also contribute to division and argument as well as commonality and solidarity. So media events that attract ritualistic attention can act as sites on which different audiences can see different ideas being celebrated. Political conventions are heavily ritualized and function to display disagreement, promote change, and celebrate differences between political factions, all the while fervently claiming American consensus. Trial procedure is a ritual of adjudication that could not work if ritual's only functions were sentiment and solidarity. Lincoln (1989) provides extended discussion of a range of such examples, which, though featuring sentiment as a major social force, could not achieve the results they do without accompanying emphasis on discourse and cognition.

It is clear that rituals have cognitive functions and thereby participate in a greater variety of social processes than would be predicted of the celebration of solidarity alone.

4.4

Maintenance of the Status Quo

It is often said that rituals function to maintain the status quo social order, and that is often true; however, it is not necessarily so, and it is not a function served exclusively. (Some authors use "ceremony" for status quo preserving rituals, and "rite" or "ritual" for transformative rituals, such as rites of passage; e.g., B. Alexander, 1987.)

Often rituals are seen as expressions of a social order that also have positive affective functions. In expressing a social order and increasing people's positive feelings about it, the ritual reinforces it. Ritual works similarly for certain cognitive functions. To the extent a ritual expression of a social order works to naturalize or preserve the taken-for-granted status of a given definition of reality, it also inhibits attempts to change that social order. This order maintaining function of ritual is common and important, but it works through complex mechanisms by which the order maintained may or may not be the sociopolitical status quo, and by which conflict and change may be promoted as well.

To the extent rituals promote ideals and ideals are not the same as actualities, they serve as evaluations and reminders of what is preferred, though neither agreement among the members of the community nor approval of the status quo are presumed. In this way ritual works as a social steering mechanism; J. C. Alexander's (1984, 1988a) analyses of the Watergate political crisis are an example.

Rituals are not so often about the way the world is as the way it is thought that it ought to be. When a minister says "love is never jealous," it is not a description of the world but a moral injunction, a prescription for action. When a president-elect swears to serve the people, it is not a description but a promise. There is often a tension between the "propositional claims" of a ritual and our experiences of everyday life. This observation can be used to portray ritual (or myth) as a form of lying (Barthes, 1957/1972; Farrell, 1989) or as a form of exploitive social control (Bloch, 1989). But it is also true that this opens the possibility of ritual being used to challenge the status quo, as in liberation theology (Tiryakian, 1988). To the extent ritual helps to maintain ideal standards, against which realities can be found wanting, ritual provides a rationale for, and may participate in, processes of social change.

Rituals, like all other communication forms, are also open to interpretation. Ritual cannot always and only function to maintain the status quo because the multivocality of dominant rituals in modern societies allows them to be used against the status quo. Frederick Douglass's (1852/1996) famous Fourth of July address opens with praise for the ideals and heroes of the American holiday. But then asks:

> What, to the American slave, is your 4th of July? I answer; a day that reveals to him, more than all other days of the year, the gross injustice and cruelty to which he is the constant victim. To him, your celebration is a sham; your boasted liberty, an unholy license; your national greatness, swelling vanity; your sounds of re-joicing are empty and heartless; your denunciations of tyrants, brass fronted impudence; your shouts of liberty and equality, hollow mockery . . . bombast, fraud, deception, impiety, and hypocrisy. (pp. 118-119)

The remainder of the speech devastatingly turns the ideals celebrated in the holiday to a critique of the failure of the society celebrating it, to live up to them.

Douglass's speech is a model of eloquent plain speaking. Another category of ritualized communication takes advantage of the multivocality of symbolic forms for more indirect speech, hiding challenges to the dominant social order. Scott (1990) reviews the great variety of ritual communication forms by which dominated people can perform civility toward the powerful, while preserving their cognitive freedom for disrespect. The spirit of such forms is indicated by the Ethiopian proverb he uses as an epigraph: "When the great lord passes the wise peasant bows deeply and silently farts" (p. v). So long as the resistance goes no farther than a silent fart, the ritual of civility does preserve the status quo. The ability to perform such rituals while actively believing their apparent opposite, however, preserves a space for free thinking that can support the emergence of resistance, conflict, and change.

Social conflict is also often ritually structured, in at least two forms. First is the ritual expression of recurrent conflicts—for example, between Indian-heritage and Spanish-heritage peoples in Mexico or between Mexican Americans and Anglos in the U.S. Southwest. In such cases of important and enduring conflicts, ritual forms evolve for conducting episodes, which are then not understood as idiosyncratic acts but are coded as instances of the larger conflict. Ritual used in these ways does maintain an order, but it is an order of conflict (e.g., Chaffee,

1993; Dirks, 1988; Foley, 1990; Gluckman, 1955, 1963; E. Hunt, 1977; P. Smith, 1991). A second type of ritually structured conflict appears in more episodic and anti-institutional events. Sit-ins, protest marches, burning effigies, verbal threats, chanting, and so on, are all performances patterned to symbolically effect the serious life—to refer back to our definition of ritual. Here again, the ritual structure is expressing and maintaining a social order, but it is an order of protest, an expression of dissention. In such situations, the ritual expresses and constitutes the social order of an oppositional group—or performs the group's denigration of the established order—and does not work for the maintenance of the status quo (L. Hunt, 1988; Ozouf, 1976/1988; Rothenbuhler, 1988a; Tiryakian, 1988; Turkle, 1975). In both of these cases the conflict is clearly understood and readily expressed. Collins (1988a; cf. Della Fave, 1991) also addresses examples in which ritual structures are mechanisms for latent social control and largely unspoken conflicts of interest in routines of everyday interaction, as in gendered divisions of labor and gendered distinctions of personal style. This is a topic I will address later.

5

Some Special Problems in the Study of Ritual

5.1

Social Change

The explanation of change is recognized as a difficulty for the student of ritual, and for the system theories with which ritual studies have historically been associated. As forms of behavior, rituals are very slow to change. They are also usually associated with ideas about tradition, stability, and order across the generations. Often their only justification is that that is the way things have always been done. As M. Wilson (1972) notes,

> the force of ritual comes partly from its antiquity, real or supposed, and the problem facing all who celebrate rituals in a fast-changing society is how to combine relevance to changing circumstances with the sanctity of tradition. (p. 188)

Though it does not necessarily follow, the study of ritual has been predominantly associated with a particular version of the study of social structure defined as synchronic inquiry into relatively stable patterns. This was British social anthropology in its era of world dominance (e.g., Fortes & Evans-Pritchard, 1940; Malinowski, 1922/1953; Radcliffe-Brown, 1922, 1952/1965; see also Harris, 1968; Leach, 1982). Ritual is conceived as symbolic expression of social order and presumed to be stable, as is the social order. The anthropological method involved reading back and forth between ritual and social orders (Bloch, 1989, esp. pp. 1-18, offers an exemplary critique). Whether this formulation resulted in a disinterest in social change or an inability to deal with social change depends on whom you ask. Either way, it is not a system of thinking that weathered the dissolution of the colonial empires particularly well.

Many references could be given for the breakdown of the synchronic ritual = social-structure system of ideas, and contrary to the tone of most critics, many of those references would be to the work of British social anthropologists striving to overcome recognized weaknesses of their own theories: Malinowski wrote a major book on cultural change (1945); Evans-Pritchard (1962, 1965, 1981) became a critic, working in a more humanistic mode, exploring cultural particularism—interestingly praised for that by some (Douglas, 1980) and criticized by others (Harris, 1968, pp. 542-543), while others denied it was true (Gellner, 1981, pp. x-xvi); Firth (e.g., 1963) has argued that the tradition never was as thoroughly synchronic as its critics paint it and that, at any rate, diachronic work has grown in prevalence and importance.

The *locus classicus,* the standard citation for the realization within the British school that the synchronic model was too simple to work, is Leach's (1954) *Political Systems of Highland Burma.* Leach was a student of Malinowski and arrived in Burma "intending to do a year's field-work and present my results as a functionalist study of a single community" (p. 311); to wit, a synchronic study of system stability. Four days later, World War II began. Leach did spend more or less a year studying a selected community before the war swept over the area and his career, but nothing was the same after that.

Leach became an officer in the Burmese army for the next five years. He traveled, recruiting native soldiers, led units in advance and retreat, and was transferred. All of his field notes and photographs and at least one finished field report were lost. Some material was rewritten from memory. The whole of the experience put him in contact with many more villages, in different cultural areas, over a larger geographic area, under different circumstances than ordinarily experienced by anthropologists interested in "a functionalist study of a single community"—not to mention the cataclysmic toll on human life and rearrangement of the relations of the nation states resulting from the war, including Burma's position in the British empire.

Under the circumstances, Leach could not ignore history nor social change. Even lacking good historical records, he could not proceed straightaway with a synchronic study as Radcliffe-Brown (e.g., 1952/1965) advised the anthropologist in search of theory to do. Rather, the book presented the complexity of the matter—that the societies the anthropologist was studying were not stable, but changing; they were not unitary, but mixed and multiple; they were not closed systems in a fixed environment (societies without history, in Wolf's (1982) apt phrase) but characterized by mixtures and interminglings of social forms and communities. Likewise, the rituals the anthropologist studied were both changing themselves and participating in the larger social change.

Conceptually loosening the identity of social orders and ritual actions, and separating both from questions of stability may seem a small breakthrough. Scholars such as Weber whose work addressed the written history of institutional religions rather than the ethnographic study of disparate societies, never imagined that rituals did not change and that they did not participate in processes of social change (e.g., Gerth & Mills, 1946/1958, pp. 267-359, 396-494). But a breakthrough it was, and the study of both changes in ritual procedures and the participation of ritual in larger social changes is common in the more recent literature.

Evidence of changing rituals and rituals in social change is available in at least four forms. First, there is an anthropological literature on culture contact and the diffusion of cultural forms from one social group to another (e.g., the diffusion of the horse among North American Indian groups) that includes consideration of changing ritual forms (e.g., Firth, 1963, pp. 80-121; Hunter, 1936; Malinowski, 1945; Turner, 1957; G. Wilson & M. Wilson, 1945; M. Wilson, 1972).

Second, the history of any institution provides instances of change in ritual and attendant institutional changes. The history of any organized religion is filled with cases. The Protestant Reformation, for example, was both about, and essentially worked out through, change in ritual form (Thomas, 1971). More recent controversies over liturgical reform in the Catholic church provide examples of both change in ritual and ritual expression of change (e.g., Dinges, 1987). Histories of political institutions demonstrate the same sorts of things (Barker, 1979; Cannadine & Price, 1987; Hobsbawm & Ranger, 1983; Hutton, 1994; Neville, 1994; Wilentz, 1985; Zei, 1995). Histories of manners and dress also show both changes in ritual form and the participation of ritual in institutional changes (Bremmer & Roodenburg, 1991; Elias, 1939/1978, 1939/1982, 1969/1983; Kasson, 1990; Koziol, 1992). The social revolution in America remembered as "the sixties" was importantly marked by changes in the form of presentation of self, of interpersonal deference and demeanor and of the codes of respect, authority, and order (e.g., Cmiel, 1994).

Third, revolutions are always accompanied by efforts to overthrow the rituals of the old regime and establish new rituals appropriate to the new social order.

Durkheim (1912/1965, e.g., pp. 474-479) discussed this briefly, using examples from the French Revolution (cf. Ozouf, 1976/1988). In that case, new calendars, holidays, saints, statues, forms of greeting, personal emblems, and new forms of meeting accompanied the new forms of government. Zei (1995) shows how the symbolic forms for marking the government—coins, flags, street names, statues—changed with the government in Slovenia throughout the 20th century; others reviewed in Chapter 10 discuss the same issues for a variety of societies throughout history. As Geertz (1977; see also Shils, 1975) points out, such ritual forms do not only accompany and mark the government and its power, they constitute it. So changes in government must be accompanied by change in ritual.

Fourth, reflection on interpersonal relationships and family life shows that as these small social orders change, so do the ritual forms of the relation (Bossard & Boll, 1950; Cheal, 1988; Reiss, 1981; Rosenthal & Marshall, 1988; Sigman, 1991). As the relationship between parent and child changes with age-grade, physical condition, social position, and economic status, so do the communication forms in which that relationship is conducted. As acquaintances become friends, as simple friendships become deeper and more complex, as romances bud and bloom and become mature relations or fade away, all of this is conducted in appropriate ritual forms of communication.

What is going on here? Two things, both important and somewhat obvious but also subtle and tricky. First, ritual and social order are not the same thing; they must have some independence or else we could not talk of them being in relation, as we clearly do when we say that ritual is a symbolic expression of the social order. So long as they are not identical, then it is logically possible for ritual to change or not to change, independent of its associated social orders—indeed the historical record is full of instances.

Second, the relation between ritual and social order is typically so tight that a reading of ritual has often been used as evidence of the social order. A member of the Kangaroo Clan is one who acts as a member of the Kangaroo Clan. The queen is identifiable, because she is treated as such. The people who wait to be introduced, avert their gaze, and dip their heads are the members of lower status. And so on. This relationship between ritual and social order is a peculiar one. It is not clear whether the ritual expresses the social order, constitutes it, or both (cf. Bell, 1992). Geertz (1980) and Goffman (1976) say the two worlds fuse, and Carey (1988) follows them but, except in special circumstances, this probably overstates the case. Perhaps the best solution, in the spirit of Burke (1961/1970, 1966, 1989), is just to say that the ritual form is a means of conducting the social order. It is one of the ways in which order is achieved.

There is a tendency to think of social order as a singular stability. It would seem that if ritual is a means of conducting the social order, then it must be singular and stable itself, and it would therefore be a force in social stability, not in social change. But this does not necessarily follow.

Real societies are not singular, stable orders but complex intermixings of various messy systems. Every small pattern of order in such a mixture will have its own ritual forms. The diffusion of those forms is one of the major mechanisms of social change: Think of the Reformation or the Renaissance, think of the changes in communication form that were part of the scientific revolution, of the establishment of legislative forms of government, of the spread of matrix organization in businesses, of quality circles, of computers and electronic messaging. In such a model of society-as-mixtures rather than society-as-system, ritual is a force of social change precisely because it is associated with social order. The U.S. Constitution, for example, banned titles of nobility, established new weights and measures to replace the British royal system, and in other ways used ritual power to effect a new social order.

Attention to the participation of ritual in social change depends on historical thinking about historical evidence. Earlier generations of anthropologists were taught not to work that way, but the shift to historical thinking throughout the human sciences may be the most important intellectual development of the last two decades. Kelly and Kaplan (1990) review that shift in the anthropological literature, tracing its roots to the shift of perspective from the study of ritual form to the study of ritual process by the young Victor Turner, among others, in the 1950s (cf. B. Alexander, 1991). To the extent communication scholars have always been more interested in process than form, we should be in a good position to contribute to this ongoing work.

5.2

Inventing Rituals

Rituals, like all social conventions, must at some point be invented, though this is at odds with the usual presentation of them as timeless. Though rituals must have some origin, it is probably rare that their invention corresponds with our images of either Edison in his laboratory or Shakespeare at his desk. Rather, the origin of rituals is usually diffused across people, places, times, and, perhaps this is key, interests. When such is not the case, when a particular person, group, or institution can be identified as the author of the ritual, and especially when the ritual is aligned with their practical interests, then most observers will be suspicious of its authenticity. At the very least, such rituals have been stripped of their indigenous, natural appearance (see Hobsbawm & Ranger, 1983, for examples of this sort of analysis).

Awareness of arbitrary foundations threatens to disauthenticate ritual both because of a distrust of symbols in general (see secs. 6.4 & 6.5; Peters & Rothenbuhler, 1989; Rothenbuhler, 1988b) and because of the need for either a little mystery or willing illusion for the felicitous performance of ritual (cf. Grimes, 1990).

Rituals and formal institutions are clearly associated. The potential for institutional advantage in ritual is obvious, so periodically, institutional actors get a notion to invent a particularly practical ritual or to attach themselves, for practical purpose, to an already established and authentic ritual. Budweiser advertisements model themselves on Olympic themes (Farrell, 1989); Coca-Cola, Inc. boasts of its honorable tradition of Olympic sponsorship; Ted Turner invents the Goodwill Games; new management theories propose organizational ritual as a means of employee control. It is easy to poke fun, and critique is often needed. But on a smaller scale the same invention of ersatz traditions and rituals is a commonplace: Aunt Edna accidentally brings lime jello with pears to the family picnic three years in a row, and then discovers everybody else thought it was a tradition. Families eat dinner together for practical reasons, but if someone is late or missing, even if for practical reasons, it feels as if a ritual were violated.

The point is that people—both as individuals and as institutions—are inventing rituals and traditions all the time, or at least they are ritualizing, that is, accentuating the ritual aspects of things. Indeed, if ritual is an element of all social action, then it is always there waiting to be accentuated, waiting for someone to invest their attention and make something more meaningful of the whole. At the level of institutions, this is just as reasonable and has yet further grounds.

As Ozouf (1976/1988) says of the festivals of the French Revolution: "The festival was an indispensable complement to the legislative system, for although the legislator makes the laws for the people, festivals make the people for the laws," (p. 9). Despite the indispensable complement between ritual and institution, it does not follow that the institution can control the ritual to its own ends:

> For the spectacle of the festival to work its spell, one must be willing to give oneself to it; one's heart must be in it. But for those who resist the spell of illusion, the whole machinery creaks; the effects become tawdry, incongruous, ridiculous. (Ozouf, 1976/1988, p. 2)

One is only likely to give one's heart to a ritual in the proper context. As Ozouf demonstrates, the great effluence of ceremonial inventiveness during the French Revolution had its motivating intellectual and social context. It also sank without a trace when the revolutionary period was over. Indeed, even during the revolutionary period, the festivals invited wildly varying reactions from contemporary intellectuals, leaving a famously ambiguous historical record. The supporters of the festivals nominate very few as excellent examples; most festivals failed to draw much attention at all: "The Revolutionary mania for festivals is the story of an immense disillusionment" (Ozouf, 1976/1988, p. 11).

Cannadine (1983) makes similar points in reviewing the ambiguous history of royal ritual in Britain. Rituals develop in historical circumstances and participate in the same processes of social change as any other symbolic form. The supposedly ancient Scottish traditions of kilt, clan-identified tartan, bagpipes, and Scottish culture heroes were invented in the century or so following 1725, by a combination of entrepreneurs, charlatans, self-deluded mystics, and innocent romantics with the leisure time to dress in kilts and imagine they were maintaining ties to their cultural past (Trevor-Roper, 1983). The modern Olympic Games were invented primarily by Coubertin, who devoted much of his adult life to the idea, at great personal expense and no clear gain, because he thought the ceremonies would have a beneficial effect on modern life (MacAloon, 1981). The Olympic flame is one of the most popular elements of the games today, and though it can be rhetorically identified with ancient origins, it was Nazi ideology that impelled the addition of a flame ceremony to the 1936 Berlin games, and the U.S. Olympic Committee has added a corporate-sponsored parade of the flame around the country as a fund-raising promotion (Slowikowski, 1991). But no matter what their origins, the flame ceremony, the Olympic Games of which it is a part, the Scottish kilt and bagpipe for those who hear their call, work because of how they are received. This is a communication problem.

6

Communication Theory
and Ritual Problems

R itual is defined as the voluntary performance of appropriately patterned behavior to symbolically affect or participate in the serious life. This chapter elucidates some principles and implications of communication theory relevant to understanding that definition. The first half of the chapter takes the form of a propositional argument, leading to the conclusion in section 6.6 that ritual is one of the strongest forms of communicative effectiveness. The second half of the chapter analyzes successive layers of the communicative properties of ritual (e.g., symbols, performed by someone, with reference to things not materially present, and so on) to arrive at an understanding of the peculiar power of ritual communication.

6.1

Ritual Is a Communicative Form

All forms of ritual are communicative. Rituals are always symbolic behaviors in social situations; therefore, they are always as if written to be read. Whatever else it may be, ritual is always also a way of saying (Leach, 1968).

However we may reduce the definition of ritual, we cannot go further than that it is a form of behavior with nonintrinsic significance. Ritual is made of body movements, cast in particular forms or patterns, that have significance, or meaning, independent of whatever is materially accomplished by the body movements themselves. The movements of ritual are signs of something else, and whatever they accomplish as rituals is accomplished by those signs and not by the movements qua movements. The baring of teeth by a dog, for example, materially accomplishes very little but signifies much. The same is true of crossing oneself, shaking hands, or swearing in presidents.

The communicative characteristics by which ritual behaviors signify, then, are primary characteristics, essential to the ritual as ritual. In that case, it is not just that rituals may have communicative functions but that if they do not function communicatively, they do not function at all.

6.2

The Effective Mechanisms of Ritual Are Communicative Devices

If what distinguishes ritual from ordinary behavior is the way in which its form signifies meaning beyond the behavior itself, what distinguishes ritual effectiveness from ordinary behavioral effectiveness must be its dependence on that signifying. Ritual effectivity, then, must work through communicative devices. If the initiation makes the girl a woman, the wedding a woman into a wife, it is via the constitutive power of symbols, speech acts, persuasion, and so on. The effectiveness of rituals has nothing essential to do with the cause and effect of mass and energy (Bateson, 1972/1987; Lévi-Strauss, 1958/1963); it is not a behavioral phenomenon (Schudson, 1989). Rather, it has to do with things being worked out, in the logic of sign systems, as understood in terms of human meaning, morality, and habit. When we say "please pass the salt" and the salt is passed, it is because of human understanding, purpose, habit, and cooperation (Pencil, 1976).

There are many important implications of the communicative nature of ritual; a general one is that we should expect that rituals work in the way that communication works. Ritual is, then, subject to the vagaries and vicissitudes of human volition, of efforts and choices, of interpretation, of attention, bias, and misunderstanding. Ritual, from this view, is not so much a holy power external to human affairs with irresistible influence over them, as something people do. Sometimes they do it well, with extraordinary effort and concentration, sometimes they do not. Sometimes they do it for admirable purposes, sometimes for condemnable reasons. In this view, ritual is not only something ordinary and human but, among the ordinary human things, it is specifically one of those by which we say things. As what we say must be interpreted by others before it can have any effect, the results can be surprising. Ritual, too, must be interpreted before it can have effect, and so necessarily, its results will depend on the sometimes surprising range of possible interpretations.

6.3

Ordering (and Other) Effects of Ritual Are Subject to the Vicissitudes of Communication

One of the most important issues of ritual study has been the relation of ritual and social order. Ritual is seen as an expression of social order that has the power to constitute it, and therefore functions in creating, maintaining, and adapting it. But if the effectiveness of ritual is constrained by the vicissitudes of communication, then so must the social ordering effects of ritual.

One of the most important issues here is that the meaning of any given ritual is subject to the interpretations of its participants, witnesses, and those who remember it. These interpretations are accomplishments of individuals that may follow effortful hermeneutic principles, but only so far as the individuals concerned choose so. Even then, interpretations are always autobiographical efforts and so arise within group membership, social position, personal history, and as part of personal and social projects. Interpretations are pre-judged (Gadamer, 1960/1975, pp. 235-274).

Here are a few examples:

The speeches, ideas, and image of Abraham Lincoln are available for ritual use by speakers of any American political party.

Within any given political speech, ritual reference to freedom will mean different things to the business owner and the laborer, the European American and the African American.

The political conventions of the Republican and Democratic parties are highly ritualized affairs; for the members of the two different parties, watching them on television is a celebration of two different kinds of solidarity, with and against.

Though huge numbers of people pay the Olympic Games a high degree of regard, it is clear that different groups regard them as celebrations of different ideas. Some see playing by the rules and friendship between competitors, athletic excellence or symbols of excellence in general, some see international cooperation, others see nationalism, the equality of the sexes (relative to other televised sport) or their differences, the superiority of African Americans over European Americans or an enactment of the ideal of American unity, and a great variety of others (Emerson & Perse, 1995; MacAloon, 1981, 1984a, 1989; Rothenbuhler, 1988c, 1989, 1995).

A new executive conducts herself so as to perform authority; some see her as competent and successful, others see her as pushy—this difference arising in confusion of the ritualized symbolics of authority and gender.

6.4

Symbolic Effectivity Is Real Effectivity

If we are to understand rituals adequately as part of the way social systems work, and rituals work through sign and meaning systems, then we must take the effectivity of signs and meanings seriously. On an ordinary level, of course, no one doubts that communication is useful for doing things: "Please pass the salt" usually results in the salt being passed. The idea of speech acts also, if relatively narrowly defined, is no longer controversial. "You're out" hollered by the right person under the right circumstances does not *refer* to your being out, but *makes* you out. Similarly "I do" under the right circumstances does not only refer to an act, but *is* the act (see Austin, 1962/1975; Finnegan, 1969; Searle, 1969; Tambiah, 1968).

Other things like speech acts are going on in communication all the time. The performance of courteousness *is* courteousness. The symbols of power are part of the exercise of power. The trappings of office are part of the nature of office. Within the limits set by the acceptance or rejection of the others with whom one shares a social situation (see Goffman, 1959, 1967), when one comports oneself as a type of person, one is that type of person. Everyone, of course, is many types of people and comports themselves differently in different situations, including as sophisticated mixtures of roles. That only complicates the fact that who we are is symbolically constructed and displayed, or more trenchantly, we are symbolically conducted.

The potential of symbols to affect physiology would appear to be the strongest test case of symbolic effectivity. So Lévi-Strauss's (1958/1963, pp. 167-205) accounts of shaman curing have become common reading in courses on ritual. It seems a certain young man set out to show that shamans were shams. He apprenticed himself, learned the techniques of hiding objects in his mouth, spitting blood at the right times, and so on. Then he set out to expose his colleagues.

What he discovered instead was that he now had curing power and that the people expected him to use it wisely. Lévi-Strauss's analysis is that the curing power of shaman ritual depends on proper performance by the shaman, including good drama, the community gathering around the patient and the shaman in support of the attempt to cure, and a belief system that integrates patient, shaman, community, and the possibility of a cure.

There are two lessons: One is the obvious one that ritual and symbol, in the right social circumstances, can cure the sick. The other has a more general theoretical importance; though these things depend on the individual, the individual is not in complete control. The cure depends on the shaman's performance, but the shaman is not free to perform in any old way. Everyone may choose the elements of their performances from what is available in their situations, but they do not choose their situations nor the rules of their performances (to adapt Marx's famous line about history). Part of the effectivity of symbols depends on their being social things that possess us as much as we possess them. To quote J. Goody (1961, p. 146) again, "the two meanings of convention, an assembly and a custom, are not accidental."

If the effects of symbols on physiology are an important test case, then we should not depend for evidence on remote cultures. As Parsons (1951/1964, pp. 439-447) points out, being sick is a social role with normative expectations just like any other (see also Carstairs, 1966). One of those expectations is that we desire to be cured, another is that scientific medicine performed by a doctor is adequate to the task. Without that symbolic definition of the situation, no cure could be effected. Carey (1988) points out that worries give us ulcers all the time; even if medical science comes to prefer another explanation, worries will remain physiologically agitating. What more intimate evidence of the effectivity of symbols could we need?

6.5

Socially Constructed Reality Is Real Reality

If one misses the point that the individual is not in control, then it becomes difficult to take symbolic effectivity seriously, for it appears to have irrational or empirically incorrect implications. If symbols effect things, and symbols depend on human performance, then it would appear individual people have that power. Two slippery spots are waiting here to be stepped in: solipsism and the condemnation of the arbitrary.

The grosser error is less common these days. Few still mistake the observation that realities are symbolically constructed for the notion that any individual can construct any reality he or she chooses. The power of symbolic construction might be logically in the hands of people, but that does not put it practically in the hands of an individual. Symbolically constituted realities are just as much a part of the environment that a given individual must adapt to as are physical realities. Our languages, cultures, traditions, social roles, and so on are given to us; we are natives in this land, not creators of it.

The second error is perversely common. Once it is noted that some element of reality has a social foundation, that it is a symbolic or a socially constructed reality, it begins to be treated as a second class reality. Since symbols have arbitrary relations with their referents and experience teaches that arbitrariness is an opportunity for duplicity and bad intent, then the socially constructed reality is treated as less authentic, less really real. This is logically indefensible and has the unfortunate implication that the only thing that can be trusted is brute physicality (see Peters & Rothenbuhler, 1989; Rothenbuhler, 1988b).

Treating symbolic realities as second class is an instance of the general tendency to dichotomize appearance and reality, image and substance, sign and referent, expression and the thing expressed (e.g., MacAloon, 1982; 1984a). Presumably, there is some dark reality dressed up as ritual; those who do the dressing are not so much engaged in ritual work as in subterfuge; Bloch (1989, pp. 19-45) says that the function of ritual is to hide reality. But this view, no matter how politically apt in a given case, is in general, communicatively naive. Ritual, just as any communicative form, owes its nature to the fusing of ideas and material forms of expression, individual interpretations and collective structures of languages, symbols, and meanings, the particularities of the communicative situation and the generalities of tradition and culture. Dichotomizing image and substance cripples our understanding of communication, and of ritual.

6.6

Within the Limits of Communicative
Effectiveness, Ritual Is a Strong Form

If the reality of social construction is understood adequately, so that the socially constituted is recognized as a structural phenomenon for the individual, if symbolic effectivity is understood adequately, so that it is recognized that even within the vicissitudes of interpretation things are affected by the use of symbols, then it is clear that ritual must be a strong form of communicative effectiveness.

By comparison with most communication, the forms of ritual are relatively invariant. So are the interpretations that, though structured by all of the particularities of any communication situation, are still mostly traditional. Add to this the fact that ritual is usually about primordial things, making use of the most deeply encoded logics of our sign and meaning systems, built on the most basic beliefs and values, most of these structures lost to consciousness from the earliest stages of our socialization. Taken together, these features of ritual give it a greater opportunity to be effective than almost any other communicative form.

That logical conclusion may be clear, but how does it work? What are the communicative properties of ritual that lend it this power? It has not received the systematic study it deserves, but a few studies have addressed the formal features of communication in ritual, the communication techniques and devices by which rituals have their effects (Bloch, 1975, 1989, pp. 19-45; Gregory, 1994; Knuf, 1994; Kuipers, 1990; Young-Laughlin & Laughlin, 1988). The second half of this chapter lays some groundwork for further communication analysis of ritual.

6.7

Symbolicity and Generality

All human communication, including rituals, is constructed of signs, such as words, gestures, flags, or pictures. These signs, as Peirce (1932) put it, are things that stand for something they are not, to someone, for some purpose. The usefulness of signs depends on their capacity to stand for something other than themselves. Words in sentences, for example, are not the things we take them to mean—they are patterns of ink on paper, luminescence on a computer screen, or vibrations of sound in air—but when used for communication they are taken to have a relationship with the things they mean. Because this relationship between the signs and the things for which they stand is at the center of human uses of signs, it is useful to distinguish three types of signs, according to the nature of this relationship: indexes, icons, and symbols.

If the "thing which stands" is the signifier, and the "thing for which it stands" is the signified, then: Indexes can be defined as signs that depend on a causal relationship between signifier and signified; icons can be defined as signs that depend on a relationship of resemblance between signifier and signified; and symbols can be defined as signs that depend on a relationship of convention between signifier and signified (Peirce, 1932). To extend a classic example: smoke is an index of fire because it is caused by it, smoke in a movie is an icon because it resembles smoke in the audience's experience, and smoke signals are symbols because the relationship between the pattern of smoke and the message is a social convention.

Here is a more complex example. The movement of the needle of a test instrument is an index of the flow of electricity through its circuits. If the dial is arranged so, then movement *up* could be an icon of an increase in whatever is being measured. Reading numbers of units of measure from the dial crosses the line to the symbolic, even though it depends on the same indexical and iconic uses. If the test instrument is used as part of a stage set for a theatrical production or part of an office decor, then it can be a symbol of technical knowledge, for example, regardless of any indexical or iconic uses. Similarly, if someone looks around an office to see what kind of place they are in, then their interpretations of the test instruments they see would be symbolic, no matter how those instruments might be used by workers in the office.

Notice that indexical signifiers are directly dependent on their particular signified: This smoke indicates this fire; this needle movement indicates this flow of electricity. Icons, though, depend on a general pattern rather than a particular relationship: This smoke is like smoke in general; this movement up resembles increase in general. Symbols, radically more so than icons, open a world of possibilities by breaking free of all particularities. The numbers and units of measure on the dial of the test instrument bring the needle movement into the system of arithmetic where it is not this number 11 that matters but the ways in which all number 11s are the same. The test instrument on the theater set does not have to be used, turned on, plugged in, or even operational because it is not this instrument that matters but the set of conventional associations with instruments in general.

These observations on the nature of indexes, icons, and symbols, especially their particular or general relation to their signified, are important for understanding how ritual works.

The stuff of ritual is largely symbolic. Though indexes and icons are often involved, symbols are the most common type of sign in ritual and usually predominate in importance. "Since symbol depends upon convention, habit or agreement, it refers not to a single instance alone, as does an index, but to a general class of instances" (Firth, 1973, p. 62). So ritual is about the general, in a significant way. Ritual action is action oriented toward transcendence of the particularities of the situation in which it is performed. A ritual situation is one constructed so as to offer transcendence of the particularities of the social circumstances surrounding it.

Presidential inaugurations are more similar than the presidencies they inaugurate (Bellah, 1970; Gronbeck, 1986; Hoxie, 1993); funerals and funeral orations are more similar than the people they help bury (Cressy, 1990; Metcalf & Huntington, 1991; Ochs, 1993). Why? Because in both cases, as in most rituals, the emphasis is on what is generally true, what has transcendent value, rather than on what is particularly true this time around. Importantly, such is inherent in the nature of symbols. As a type of sign, the symbol depends on generalization for its meaning, and promotes generalization in its interpretation.

6.8
Materiality and Indexicality

But rituals also always have an indexical component. Communication, including ritual, always brings together inner and outer worlds by the shaping of material to express an idea. The material element of communication must work through causal mechanisms. A voice can be heard or not because of the nature of sound energy; a newspaper can be read or not because of the physical processes of printing and distribution. In turn, these material elements and their causal connections can be interpreted as indexical signs. The volume of the voice indicates the physical energy that was invested in speaking, for example (but note that a whisper could be interpreted symbolically as a sign of great psychic energy). In the ordinary flow of communication we pay indexes relatively little regard; their primary use is probably for orientation, or checking facts—as in turning attention from one speaker to another, or checking to see who said what.

What makes ritual special in this regard is that its performative aspect gives the essential, but ordinary, indexical element of all communication a special importance. The fact that "most symbolic behavior must work through the human body" (Douglas, 1970/1982, p. vii) is a fundamental that should not be overlooked in any communication study; it takes on special importance in rituals because they are performances. Because indexes do not have the arbitrariness of connection between signifier and signified that symbols do, they are neither as flexible in use as symbols, nor as unreliable. Performance in a ritual is an index of relationship vis-à-vis the canon, the liturgy, the meaning of the ritual that is usually carried by symbols. Hence, the index of performance is a prop of ensurance against the potential indeterminateness of meaning, intention, belief, and other symbolically embodied phenomena (Rappaport, 1979, pp. 173-221, 223-246). Note that ritual is not different from ordinary communication in this regard; our performance of a conversational turn indicates that we said it. But the social importance of that indication is of a different category in ritual, because the performance is according to ritual form, and therefore a form of participation in the serious life.

The ritual cannot be performed without bodily participation. Of course it cannot be performed correctly without that bodily participation being according to form. As the ritual is a kind of speech act, its effectiveness depends on its correct or, as Austin (1962/1975) more cheerfully puts it, felicitous, performance. (Note that the criterion of felicity allows improvisation whereas the criterion of correctness usually would not. This is one way that rituals could be categorized, according to their dependence on felicity or correctness, and hence the degree to which they are dominated by a liturgy or their contemporary circumstances.) For Durkheim (1912/1965),

> [t]his is the explanation of the fundamental importance laid by nearly all cults upon the material portion of the ceremonies. This religious formalism . . . comes from the fact that since the formula to be pronounced and the movements to be made contain within themselves the source of their efficacy, they would lose it if they did not conform absolutely to the type consecrated by success. (p. 50)

Because the performative aspect of bodily participation in the ritual is also an index of position vis-à-vis the meaning and effects of the ritual, the surprising result is that a participant cannot lie in ritual, or at least cannot ritually lie (Rappaport, 1979, pp. 173-221, 223-246; cf. Zuesse, 1987). Participants may or may not believe in a ritual, but their participation in it cannot be a lie; their disbelief does not undo what was accomplished by their participation.

People may be married by a variety of ritual procedures, in a variety of institutional settings, in ceremonies that do or do not include reference to a variety of liturgies, religious beliefs, and legal powers. Each of the participants may have a variety of beliefs and doubts; their intentions may be good, bad, or indifferent. But participation in the performance of the ritual is an index of acceptance of the symbolic power of the things said and done. That symbolic power creates a married couple who will be held responsible to their status. The marriage can only be undone by another ritual procedure.

Another example: If I tip my head and gaze downward, offer my hand and my appreciation while being introduced to someone of higher social status, whether I respect that person or not, my performance indicates my acceptance of his or her higher status. If I do not offer my hand, tip my head, or express my appreciation, then I indicate my disrespect. We have very little choice in ritually charged situations—whatever is done is a performance with indexical significance. Lack of choice is also indicated by the rule that ignorance is no excuse. For example, if I do not know that someone is worthy of respect or do not know how to perform respect in the relevant social circle, then my disrespect is unintentional but still real. My actions will be read by others as an index of my incompetence, disrespect, or both. That opinion will determine the future desirability of my company in that social circle, whether it be a royal court or a tavern.

"In a ritual, the world as lived and the world as imagined, fused under the agency of a single set of symbolic forms, turn out to be the same world" (Geertz, 1973, p. 112). This is a strange consequence of materiality—and one only possible in communicative forms, because of their unique fusing of the material and ideal. In being consecrated by a group, in the material of ritual performance, imagined worlds become real. This is not a dependence on materiality to authenticate symbols; what is important about the material form here is that it is symbolic, that it is according to ideas, that what it makes real in this world is an ideal world.

6.9

Backward and Forward References

Rituals always refer in two directions: Backward, as it were, to the social order and the culture in which the ritual is embedded, and forward, as it were, to the people performing the ritual and those with whom they will interact. The backward reference is symbolic and offers the meaning of the ritual; the forward reference is more indicative and offers the immediate and soon-to-be-realized social significance of the ritual. Note that the fusing of the backward and forward references in the present may create the subjunctive mood that Turner and his school emphasize (e.g., Turner, 1969/1977, 1982a, 1982b; MacAloon, 1984b).

Students of ritual traditionally emphasize the backward reference; they talk about ritual being out of time, in a sacred space, a performance set aside from the practical exigencies of this world, and so on. This orientation is precisely what leads other scholars, such as Bloch (1989), to derogate ritual; not being of this world is identified with not being about this world, and the whole is therefore considered maladaptive, unhealthy, and dangerous. It is to the ethologists (as Goffman, 1976, points out; see sec. 4.1) that we owe the insight that ritual is also a communication form for display of alignment and orientation in a present and still unfolding social situation. Without analysis of this dimension, we lack a complete understanding of what ritual is and how it works.

Ritual, then, is about *both* position in a cosmic order and alignment in a practical world. It embeds its participants, by these two different logics, into an ongoing structure: by symbol and index, into past and future, origins and destinations, relatively stable meanings and more changeable significances. In other words, ritual is a communication device for uniting the ideal and the material, the general and the particular, the cosmic and the ordinary, the past and the future, the structures of history and the happenings of individual lives.

6.10

The Problem of the Relation of Witness and Spectator, Ritual and Spectacle

Somewhere along the way, with the complexities of life in the 20th century in Europe and America, came a great distrust of spectacle and a worry that our world was characterized by more and more of it all the time. As MacAloon (1984a) discusses, in earlier American thought a spectacle was not a bad thing, but in the 20th century, there may be no more distrusted phenomenon. Political spectacle is suspected of fascism; sports spectacles are big for the sake of bigness; a spectacular film might be a popular success, but it is too grandiose to be good art; if I make a spectacle of myself, I have reason to be embarrassed.

The spread of spectacle has been taken as evidence of debasement (e.g., Boorstin, 1961), while advocated as revolutionary strategy (e.g., Debord, 1977). Debates about the good or ill functions of the mass media center on their provision of communication or spectacle. Lazarsfeld (1940) and parents and teachers everywhere distinguish the spectator media of radio, television, and film from print media; they distrust the former, and prefer the latter.

The role of witness is often prescribed in rituals and thus constitutes a form of participation. A wedding, for example, must have witnesses. But what if a ritual has an audience that is not required to witness? Is this a significant difference in nature? Is spectating categorically opposed to participation? Is participation required for healthy outcomes? Does the presence of spectators recast the ritual as spectacle and thus make it worthy of suspicion; does it offer only the appearance of ritual, a kind of social trick, probably used to bad ends?

First it is important to remember that spectating *is* a mode of access. It has limits, so if one's participation goes no further than spectating, then the meaning of the ritual will probably be thin and its effectiveness small. But spectating can provide access to other modes of participating; it can recruit viewers to engagement of festival, ritual, and other social forms (MacAloon, 1984a). Watching the televised funeral, often in groups, was an important part of the recovery of confidence by the American public following the assassination of John F. Kennedy, as not only public opinion and worries but reported psychosomatic symptoms too, changed following the events, media coverage, and interpersonal contact (Greenberg & Parker, 1965). Studies of the television audience of the Olympics indicate that people are able to engage ceremony, festival, and ritual—with the aid of friends, food, and drink (Emerson & Perse, 1995; Rothenbuhler, 1988c, 1989, 1995). Casual observation at any football stadium or basketball arena indicates that spectatorship is no simple social category; it is associated with a great variety of forms of participation in what can be a deeply meaningful experience. Even in addition to the meanings of the experience for the crowd as spectators, there is evidence that the crowd really does play on the home team, giving them a statistically significant advantage even after controlling for other potential explanations (Schwartz & Barsky, 1977).

There is too much casualness in the use of the word spectator and in discussions of spectacle. A spectator is almost never simply looking at something. On the contrary, most forms of spectatorship are socially prescribed and performed roles and forms of communication (Anderson & Meyer, 1988; Eastman & Riggs, 1994; Lemish, 1982; Lindlof & Meyer, 1987; Lull, 1980, 1982; Renckstorf, McQuail, & Jankowski, 1996; Rothenbuhler, 1988b). The spectator is, then, not simply a viewer but a participant in a larger system. Seen through the lens of communication theory, it is clear that spectatorship is another part of certain ritual forms.

6.11

The Phenomenal Status of the Ritual Text in the Actor's Environment

To engage in a ritual is to voluntarily submit the self to an order of signs. In the prototypical ritual, the actor is a member of a community for whom the order of signs is powerful. Rituals vary in formality, of course, from relatively loose celebrations through ceremonial forms that appear as features of otherwise

informal everyday interactions to very strictly scripted occasions of the greatest
solemnity in which variance of procedure will be considered morally wrong or
even dangerous. But in all ritual there is an emphasis on form, on the sequence
of signs. The necessity of this sequence is independent of the will of the actor.
So a ritual order of signs is a condition in the environment of the actor (using
Parsons & Shils's, 1951, vocabulary of actors in environments of conditions and
resources; see also Rothenbuhler, 1987; Shepherd & Rothenbuhler, 1991).

Signs work through the will of the individual and thus there is an element
of contingency in their ordering power (Dilthey, 1976, pp. 170-263; Ricoeur,
1950/1966, 1974). The signs of a ritual, like the signs of ordinary communication, require our interpretation for their meanings to have a phenomenological
presence, and interpretation is something that is a gift of the actor, not a condition
of the situation. As Rappaport (1979, pp. 173-221) points out, there is always a
voluntaristic moment in the choice of participation in a ritual. But once that
moment is gone, no one present in the performance of a ritual chooses the syntax.
The order of the signs is as it must be and not as we choose it to be. The order
of the signs, the syntax of our performance is a condition on our will.

There are, of course, other obvious examples in which signs are conditions
of action. First, to the extent the meanings and possible uses of signs are condi-
tional on their positions in systems of signs, as it is generally understood to be
(Saussure, 1915/1966; Barthes, 1964/1968), those meanings and possible uses
are in turn conditions on our uses of those signs. However, so long as choices of
syntax are still open, this condition in the environment is primarily a resource.
It is because of the stability of sign meanings and uses across individual uses
and users that signs *are* meaningful and useful.

Second, at one level, anything said or done by another is a condition in an
actor's environment. Nevertheless, if these others are socially available, we can
interact with them, whether cooperatively or conflictually, and the things they
say and do become part of a mutually constructed social world.

Third, works of art, drama, literature, and so on are, for the audience, fixed
sign forms, objects in the environment, conditions on the willful act of interpretation. The interpreter can go to work on the text, but the textual object will not
answer, adapt, or interact. Some, such as Fish (1980), will value the work of
interpretation above the object of interpretation. But for the purposes of communication studies, it is important to remember that there *is* an object of interpretation, a physical thing existing in a physical environment, exhibiting sen-
sorily available patterns without which there would be no opportunity for the
work of interpretation. Even though the textual object will not become whatever
it is asked to be, won't bend to any and every reader's will, because the object

of interpretation is detached from its author and now independent of the will that originally shaped it, the interpreter has a freedom of interpretation unavailable in interactive social situations (see Ricoeur, 1976, 1981, pp. 145-164, 197-221). There is no one to stand and say, "that is not what I meant." So, unlike the given order of signs in ritual, the given order of signs in textual objects is usually experienced as an opportunity, a resource more than a condition.

Ritual is relatively unique among communication forms, in the extent to which it simultaneously depends on an actor's performance *and* operates as a condition on that performance, limiting the range of the actor's choices. This can be further illustrated in reference to mixed cases.

There are many text-objects for which a community sanctions only a narrow range of interpretation or response. These include things such as national anthems, tropes that regularly appear in political speeches, stories that a family tells about itself, the canons that are taught in freshman college courses, or even crime news stories. In such cases, the text-object is being treated in a more ritualistic way; the actor's experience is less of being in an audience and more of being a participant in a community.

Less common, but still a readily available example, are rituals for which community sanction has lost its power, or witnesses over whom the community sanction has no power. In such cases, the ritual is becoming a textual object, the participant a spectator. If someone attends Catholic Mass because they think the priest's robes look nifty, then the ritual is a textual object engaged for entertainment value. To the extent the postmodernists are right and irony really is the mood of the day, then some of this is what is going on. Ostensibly valuable social acts are performed for personal stimulation; questions of representation, along with transcendent value, are moot.

However, when participants operate within the order of the ritual and the sanction of the community, the syntax of the signs, and most of their interpretation, is fixed. Communication theory helps identify what a unique situation that is.

6.12

Some Implications of the Peculiar Phenomenal Status of Ritual

Rituals are not always substantively voluntary performances or representative expressions of the internal states of an actor. Rituals are also used as socialization devices, in which it is important that ritual forms can be imposed on the actor from without. Of course, rituals would not work as socialization if there were not inherent in the ritual some implication of the voluntary expression of the actor. If the importance of behavior according to ritual form could be exhausted by its social conformity, there would be no difference between it and physical coercion. In that case, the ritual would have no socializing power, for adherence to its form could only be guaranteed by the presence of an external power. Instead, in a socializing ritual, an authority introduces the idea of behavior according to ritual form, but over time that idea becomes internalized, so that actors make their own choices to behave according to form. How does that work?

The function of ritual as a form of display behavior makes the internal states of the actor public. But the socialization and subordination functions of ritual make public states internal.

Imagine an interaction conducted according to ritual form (Goffman, 1959, 1967). The actor that initiates the interaction not only offers a line that he or she proposes for self, but a line for the other as well. In the way I say hello I offer both a conception of my identity and of yours. In their being performed together, these two lines constitute a line for the relationship enacted in this interaction. My saying hello indicates who I propose to be and who I propose that you be. It is a proposal that, for the length of this interaction, we conduct our relationship as those two social identities. Subsequent interaction turns will then have the signficance, among other things, of accepting, rejecting, or amending the currently offered interaction line. These offers, acceptances, and amendations of identities are found in the ritualistic style of interaction, operating independently of what we usually think of as the substance of talk.

Now imagine an interaction conducted according to ritual form between a subordinate and a superior. The superior usually initiates the interaction and thus offers the line. The subordinate must accept the line or run the risk of insubordination—the refusal to perform the role of being subordinate. When a boss, for example, is friendlier than necessary, choices of response are pretty well constrained to being gracious or ungrateful.

Now imagine an interaction conducted according to ritual form between a subordinate and superior in a situation that has socializing outcomes, either intended or not. For example, imagine a seventh-grade math teacher interacting with students in the classroom. Differences in the manner of interaction with different students signify differences in the teacher's conception of each student. Because of the authority of the teacher, the student must either accept or carefully but persistently resist those conceptions. Resisting runs the risk of being received as insubordination—a large risk in a seventh-grade classroom. Accepting obligates the student to the performance of a role. Because we are supposed to be who our behaviors imply we are—at least in modern, Western cultures—performing a role obligates us to be it. Therefore, if the teacher consistently offers girls the line that they are people who do not understand or like math but are pretty, charming, and polite, and offers boys the line that they are rough, loud, and impolite but clever, then that is likely who they will become.

These are simple examples that cry out for detailed study of real situations, but as sketches they are sufficient to illustrate some of the implications of the peculiar phenomenal status of ritual in the world of communication. Because it appears as communication, ritual does not exist without someone's performance, and that performance operates as an index of their acceptance. Because ritual performance must be according to form, it is a more constraining presence in the environment than any other type of communication.

Part II

Ritual in Communication Research

Five Contributions
of the Ritual Concept to
Communication Studies

7.1

Renaming as a
Spur to Rethinking

The first contribution that the ritual concept can make to communication studies derives from the intellectual stimulus of renaming. Scholars often get stuck in habits of thinking; the simple act of renaming can sometimes serve as a useful spur to creativity.

What, for example, if small group decision making was identified as a ritual, rather than a rational, process? Would that produce useful rethinking? What about other areas of communication studies? This is the kind of thinking behind the Gerbner group's claim that television is the modern American religion (e.g., Gerbner & Gross, 1976; Gerbner, Gross, Morgan, & Signorielli, 1982, 1986). Gerbner and his colleagues are trying to jolt us out of old habits of thinking about what television is, how it works, what sort of effects we should expect of it, and how to go about studying it.

Naming, however, is not analysis; ritual has to make more of a contribution than this to count as an important concept. So let us move on to four other types of analytic payoff.

7.2

Help to Identify
Unanalyzed Aspects of Things

The ritual concept can help identify as yet unanalyzed aspects of things. For example, relationships are an important topic in communication studies. Usually the study of relational communication focuses on conversation. But if a ritual aspect of that relational communication were identified, then attention would be drawn to other aspects as well. The ritual aspect of conversation would be seen as one part of a larger category; researchers' attention would also be drawn to the other ritual aspects of relationship, and these too would be seen as instances of communication. What about, for example, gifts, doing favors, taking turns buying rounds of drinks, or paying for lunch as ritual performances, symbols that enact the relationship (Cheal, 1988; Otnes & Beltramini, 1996)? These forms of relational communication are as informative and as worthy of investigation as is talk.

7.3

Help to Explain
Anomalous Aspects of Things

The ritual concept can aid understanding of otherwise anomalous aspects of things. Why is so little of the conversation in interpersonal relationships informing? Why is so much time spent saying the same things, or saying nothing much at all? Perhaps it is talk structured by ritual, rather than informing, purposes, and would thus appear anomalous under a nonritual analytic frame.

Prayer is a classic example of a regularly recurring human activity that appears anomalous unless analyzed within an appropriate conceptual frame. As discussed in section 2.1.4, according to some classic definitions of rationality, ritual forms such as prayer are defined as noninstrumental, arational, or irrational action. They come to be seen as a form of magic, mystery, or misunderstanding about the causal forces at work in this world. The question, then, becomes why so many rational people repeatedly engage in these activities, claiming to benefit by doing so. Weber (1922/1978) developed the model of value-rational action— action "determined by a conscious belief in the value for its own sake of some ethical, aesthetic, religious, or other form of behavior, independently of its prospects of success" (pp. 24-25)—in order to solve this problem. Prayer may not be instrumentally rational as judged by the economist, but it is rational from the point of view of the value system of the one praying. Generalizing from this case, understanding ritual provides a conceptual frame that illuminates otherwise anomalous types and aspects of human behavior.

Studies of political protest and economic strikes, to take another example, often use rational action models to explain the strategies chosen and the outcomes obtained (e.g., McAdam, 1982; Tilly, 1978). Other studies use a conceptual framework emphasizing ritual and symbol to analyze protest strategies as communication forms (e.g., Chaffee, 1993; E. Hunt, 1977; L. Hunt, 1988; Rothenbuhler, 1988a; Tiryakian, 1988; Turkle, 1975). Repeatedly we find that there is more to strikes and protests than can be explained by the rational action models. Despite their strengths, those models cast many of the details of protest action as irrational, and thus inexplicable. However, if one thinks of a strike as a communication device that can be ritually structured to enact a vision of an alternative social order, or to degrade the existing one, then many of those same protest strategies appear sensible. They may be economically irrational or politically unstrategic, but judged as expressions of ideals, they are ritually reasonable.

7.4

Help to Form More
Appropriate Expectations of Things

Helping to form more appropriate expectations of things is another aspect of understanding anomalous aspects of things. When people's actions are structured by ritual, scholars need to be informed by thinking about ritual in forming their research questions and hypotheses. Such logic will produce more appropriate expectations than will thinking not informed by an understanding of ritual.

For example, because their usual purpose is to increase sales, advertisements appear as persuasive communication. Because decades of research have shown how persuasion works on cognitions, attitudes, and behaviors, scholars look for changes in those areas in response to advertising. But advertising may also be a ritual display of approved social roles and relations; for example, most beer commercials are not so much persuasive statements about the reasons for buying a brand of beer as they are symbolic enactments of a vision of the good life. In this case, commercials would have effects on the system of meanings, on visions of the good life, on expectations of the behavior of others, and so on. As research by Baran and Blasko (1984) shows, when we go looking for it, that is exactly what we find (see also Schudson, 1984, e.g., p. 210; Williams, 1980). When this same logic is carried over into the study of consumer behavior, attention is drawn to rituals of consumption and ritualistic effects on self-identification, relations, and meanings (Belk, Wallendorf, & Sherry, 1989; Gainer, 1995). Research that is not informed by thinking about the possible ritual functions of advertising will not be able to predict these sorts of results.

7.5

As Disciplinary Leverage

Finally, the ritual concept can be used as a kind of disciplinary leverage. It can work as a lever on our own thinking and also for our purposes in debate with the other disciplines of the human sciences.

First, as a lever on our own thinking: If we accept rituals as a form of communication and add them to our curriculum we expand the current boundaries of our field. Our attention is drawn to forms of communication that are intimately involved with social order, its maintenance and adaptation. It is likely we will come to see more of the whole scope and ubiquity of communication as an aspect of all social action and a foundation of all social processes.

Second, as a lever for our purposes in disciplinary debates: If ritual is an aspect or element of all social action, and if ritual works by communicative devices, then communication is a part of the process of all social action. There is a contribution for students of communication to make throughout the fields of the human sciences.

Here are two brief examples of the benefits we should expect. When we study sport as ritual (e.g., Birrell, 1981; Brownell, 1993; Eastman & Riggs, 1994; Foley, 1990; Riordan, 1987; Slowikowski, 1991), attention is drawn to the layer of symbolic performance for participation in the serious life that exists alongside the muscular performance and entertaining display. Sports becomes part of the field of communication studies, not just because it is on TV but because the ritual frame identifies the communicative functions of sports.

Another example comes from gender studies. Many have noted differing tendencies of female and male communication style (e.g., Gilligan, 1982; Kramarae, 1981; Lakoff, 1975). Whether to ascribe these differences to biological sex, psychological gender, sexist ideology, or some other cause continues to be a subject of debate (e.g., Coates, 1996; Crawford, 1995; Johnson & Meinhof, 1997). In most cases, though, matters of communication are cast as outcomes, explained by reference to noncommunicative facts and processes. When gendered styles of communication can be understood as matters of ritual performance (e.g., Parker, 1988), and ritual identified as essential to gendered socialization (e.g., Carnes, 1989), the social processes that produce gendered differences in communication will be seen to depend on communicative activities themselves. Then communication would be among the causes of the phenomenon, and the most appropriate understandings would come from communication scholars.

Recent literature has advocated constructionist or interactionist views, in which the ritual conception could play a useful part. Crawford (1995), for example, argues

> Women *are* different from men. Yet, paradoxically, this is not because they are women. . . . Each of us behaves in gendered ways because we are placed in gendered social contexts. . . . Therefore, if women try *not* to "do gender," they will confront the social consequences of violating these norms and expectations. (p. 16)

Collins (1988a) has proposed essentially the same idea, pointing out that it is Durkheimian in intellectual heritage. Our contributions are two: To identify this as a ritualistic interaction, with communication forms as the effective devices by which such processes operate (see secs. 6.11 & 6.12); and to shift the intellectual categories so the effective ritual communication that produces gender style differences will be seen together with the role of ritual communication in the more physiological matters of sexual initiation and reproduction rites (Lutkehaus & Roscoe, 1995; K. E. Paige & J. M. Paige, 1981).

8

Mediated Communication in Ritual Form

The possibility that mediated communication may take ritual form has been discussed in the literature in four distinct ways. This chapter reviews that research moving, in order, from the most conventional definition of ritual, through two less conventional definitions, to a fully controversial claim about the religious status of television in America today. Though this last idea is the most obviously controversial, each of the claims is debatable because anthropological ideas developed in the study of small-scale, nonindustrial societies are being applied to the production and consumption of modern, commercial media.

First, and most clearly fitting a conventional notion of ritual, are special media events in which live television coverage functions as a key part of the ceremonial event. The funeral of John F. Kennedy, the wedding of Prince Charles and Lady Diana, the funeral of Lord Mountbatten, and the travels of Pope John Paul II are examples of such occasions when the television coverage itself takes on a ceremonious style and television audiences are recruited into a form of participation at a distance. This tele-participation in the ceremony is possible only by telecommunication, and represents a distinctly modern form of ritual.

Ritualized media use is a second type of mediated communication in ritual form. It is important to distinguish ritual media use from habitual media use, as discussed in section 3.1. But certain cases of media use present clear examples of ritualization, as audience members prepare for and conduct their television viewing, record listening, sports spectating, or other activities in ways that fully correspond with the definition of ritual as appropriately patterned behavior to symbolically participate in the serious life.

Rituals of media work are the topic of a third area of research on mediated communication in ritual form. Examples include journalists' dependence on standard questions, their interest in standard topics, and their writing in standard story forms. The ritual in this case is not a ceremonial event but a formal routine of everyday work life, a symbolic method of coping with symbolic dangers. Where media events are examples of ritual by media, these are examples of media by ritual.

The fourth topic addressed in this chapter is the deservedly controversial claim that television today functions as an American religion. The argument that it does depends on identifying ritual forms in television programming and television viewing. The argument that it does not depends on the failure to identify numbers of people who take ordinary, everyday television viewing as seriously as the faithful take religion, who claim to have the same sorts of experiences in television viewing that the faithful have in religious worship.

8.1

Media Events and Mediated Rituals

Katz and Dayan have drawn attention to the fact that certain special media events function as ritual celebrations, as special time-outs from the normal for attention to the ceremonial (see Dayan & Katz, 1988, 1992; Katz, 1980; Katz & Dayan, 1986). By this, they mean more than that the media sometimes portray ritual celebrations, though that is an important part of it. The key hypothesis is that in the way certain events are sponsored by central social institutions, presented by electronic media, and received by their audience, they are constructed as and function as ritual celebrations. Therefore, they may play the role of periodic social gatherings for the celebration of society as discussed by Durkheim (Dayan & Katz, 1988, 1992; Rothenbuhler, 1988c, 1989, 1995). This is no small point, for if true, it implies there are communicative means for overcoming the presumption that people must be physically gathered together to celebrate a ritual (Rothenbuhler, 1988b, and contra MacAloon, 1984a, p. 270).

Examples of these events include state funerals and royal weddings, the astronauts' walk on the moon, Sadat's visit to Jerusalem, the Pope's trips, the Olympic Games, the Watergate hearings, political conventions and debates, election coverage, and inaugurations. There are also similar events that operate less independently of the media, attract only a small audience, or are less widely recognized as important. The broadcast of religious ritual and programming works for its audiences similarly to the way major media events work for their more general audiences (Hoover, 1988; Lutgendorf, 1990b). For some audiences, in some ways, things such as the Academy Awards presentations, the Live-Aid concert, the Eurovision Song Contest, and *The Rocky Horror Picture Show* can serve similar functions (e.g., Kinkade & Katovich, 1992). K. Becker (1995) points out that media coverage and participation in public events—press conferences, speeches, protests—can constitute a form of ritualizing as well. These, however, are not the more widely recognized special events with which Katz and Dayan are primarily concerned. Specifically excluded from the realm of media events are normal news broadcasts, drama, the less than spectacular and the less than central in Shils's (1975) sense of a geography of cultural importance. But modern societies, of course, possess many centers for many different social groups, some overlapping, some not, hence centrality, like sacredness, should always be judged from the point of view of the people for whom it counts as such.

Dayan and Katz (1992, pp. 4-14) offer a formal definition of media events. The first set of qualifications (labeled syntactic in Dayan & Katz, 1988) is that they are *interruptions* of normal broadcasting routines, presented *live, organized outside the media,* and *preplanned.* Without any one of these traits, the event in question is not the type of media event of interest here. The Kennedy assassination, for example, was a live interruption organized by someone other than the media, but it was not preplanned by the media and other legitimate institutions. The Kennedy funeral fits the definition of ceremonial media event; neither the Kennedy assassination nor the Kennedy mini-series do.

The second set of qualifications (labeled semantic in Dayan & Katz, 1988) are that media events are presented with *reverence* and *ceremony,* they aim at *reconciliation,* and are declared *historic.* (Dayan and Katz, 1992, also include that they celebrate the "*voluntary* actions of great personalities" [p. 8], but this may be characteristic of Western events and not necessary to the definition.) Note that these terms of definition move closer to the substance of particular media events, distinct from the form of events in general. Rather than ruling a phenomenon in or out of our concern, the absence of one of these qualifications would call into question the seriousness of the event or the adequacy of the presentation.

The third set of qualifications (labeled pragmatic in Dayan & Katz, 1988) is that media events *excite large audiences,* are characterized by a *norm of viewing,* give viewers reason to *celebrate, integrate* societies, and *renew loyalties.* They include *hegemonic* among the second set of qualifications because of the close connections of media events and social centers. However, that idea belongs more naturally in this third set of qualifications that emphasize results rather than meanings and, like the issue of personal voluntarism, may be characteristic of the events the authors happen to have chosen for study but not necessary to events as they could be imagined. These terms of definition address the results of media events; if one of them is not present, it calls into question the success of the event.

If some media events function as Durkheimian celebrations of social solidarity, then they should be liminal times that bear a subjunctive relationship to everyday social activities, times of heightened contact of periphery with center, of a denser presence of sacred authorities, sacred rituals, and collective representations, and a time of greater salience of the fundamental beliefs and values of the society at hand. Media events should also be celebrations, times of festivity, play, and sociability. Most of these hypotheses have received one or another degree of support. (See the research discussed in Dayan & Katz, 1992.)

There are any number of reasons to doubt these ideas about media events. On the face of it, it seems that as soon as a ritual or celebration is presented by media, it is transformed into spectacle (MacAloon, 1984a, pp. 270, see also 1982). If a media presentation is to constitute a ritual celebration, then it must somehow create a group, crowd, or functional equivalent (Rothenbuhler, 1988b); if the audience is nothing but dispersed spectators, how can they be seen as ritual participants? In the United States and elsewhere the commercial functions of the media are their most obvious attribute; at a time when the ideological functions of the media are well understood, why would we trust their presentation of ritual and celebration? Chaney (1983) makes several points regarding the presentation of ritual by media in a mass society, including the dangers of a media-constructed or media-usurped public sphere, transforming participation into spectatorship in the name of enlarging the audience.

As participants in ritual, the media also bring a new set of exigencies to the situation. Lyons and Lyons (1987) compare the ceremonies of a successful television preacher with more traditional rituals in Nigeria. The more traditional rituals were less definitely scheduled—they would start when everyone was ready—and much of the time was spent getting ready, waiting, and cleaning up. The televised rituals, on the other hand, conformed to the television schedule and were performed under the pressure to be interesting at all times. This is an instance of a general problem: Mediated ritual must adapt to standard operating practices of the media, even as the media adapt to the contingencies of special occasions. To the extent the media become one of the more powerful institutions of the situation, various other demands come into play.

What is needed is neither trust nor cynicism but careful analysis. If television and the other electronic media are dominant public communication forms, then we should expect them to perform some of the same roles that dominant public communication forms have performed in other societies. Those will include ritual and celebration.

8.2

Ritualized Media Use

Viewers of televised media events act notably different from viewers in more routine situations. In the days between the assassination and funeral of President Kennedy, people watched much larger than normal amounts of television—often in groups—and supplemented that with much interpersonal talk (Greenberg & Parker, 1965). During the Olympic Games as well, people tend to watch more television, viewers are more likely to be in a group, groups tend to be larger and are more likely to include visitors from outside the home; viewers are more likely to be eating and drinking, to be talking about what they are watching, to have planned their viewing ahead of time, and to report that they are paying special attention (Rothenbuhler, 1988c). Dayan and Katz (1992) report a variety of such instances, from television viewers standing at attention to replicating royal meals. In isolation, such examples may appear to be nothing more important than behavioral quirks. But when they are characteristic of the behavior of large numbers of people, when people report that such things are important to them, and when the behaviors fit into a meaningful pattern with associated beliefs, values, emotions, and symbolic expressions, they can be seen to be examples of fully ritualized television viewing (Emerson & Perse, 1995; Rothenbuhler, 1989, 1995).

Similar patterns can be observed among the audience for religious television (Hoover, 1988; Lutgendorf, 1990b) and among the fans of sports teams, soap operas, science fiction, and music. Anecdotal reports are common, but Wenner and Gantz (1989) documented that ritualized activities were not uncommon among sports fans watching television, including wearing team colors, consuming special foods or drinks, performing routine preparatory activities, sitting in certain chairs, or repeating certain phrases at selected times. Eastman and Riggs (1994) found that sports fans' ritualized television watching functioned to define group membership, allow them a form of participation in the event, feelings of connection with the team, each other, and the school or city the team represents, feelings of reassurance, and a partially playful, partially serious sense of influencing the outcome of the game. Periodically repeated activities, the wearing of special clothes, gathering into groups, and rearranging other social routines in order to perform an identity of group membership have been documented among fans of music, soap operas, science fiction, and film stars (e.g., Lewis, 1992). Though the seriousness of such things varies, and thus their status as rituals, many fans are very serious, and these types of activities are definitely ritualized—they are patterns whose latent ritual possibilities are being accentuated to one degree or another.

Similar possibilities exist in certain regularly repeated media forms. Vande Berg (1995) argues that television specials about John F. Kennedy can function as ritual occasions, producing symbolic pilgrimages for viewers attuned to the possibilities. Kinkade and Katovich (1992) show that the ritualistic activities of the audience for cult films such as *The Rocky Horror Picture Show,* which many dedicated viewers watched as a weekly, occasional, or annual event, operate in association with unique textual features in support of a particular world view. Because of their annual repetition and symbolic embodiment of recognizable values, annually televised films such as *The Wizard of Oz* can also become the center of family rituals (Payne, 1989).

Even everyday television possesses some potential for ritualization, because of its regular repetition if nothing else. A number of authors have commented on how the structure of the television text, across programs, produces a punctuated flow coordinatable with household activities (e.g., Altman, 1987; Modleski, 1983; Williams, 1974). Selberg (1993) shows that selected moments in that punctuated flow can be used in ritualistic ways to mark transitions from one day part to another, to mark key days of the week, and special days of the year. Watching the evening news, for example, can be part of a ritualistic transition from the work of the day to the leisure of the evening, or from a period of family separation in individual activities to a period of greater togetherness.

Across these examples, admittedly varying in degrees of seriousness and the formality and completeness of their ritual, we see examples of ritualized media use that are symbolic activities for participation in some larger order of meanings. This is ritual properly speaking, as distinct from the residual category of merely not-instrumental media use that has sometimes been labeled as ritual media use (see sec. 3.1).

8.3

Rituals of Media Work

Any number of areas of media work could be examined from a ritual studies frame, but the area that has been studied the most is newswork. In this case, the utility of ritual concepts is well established.

As an epistemology, objectivity has several problems that are well known in the academy; yet, the idea of objectivity continues to be the primary basis for the public legitimacy of journalistic reporting. Indeed, as a number of authors have shown, "objectivity" is deeply encoded in the organization and practice of journalistic work so that it serves many useful functions (e.g., Phillips, 1972; Tuchman, 1972). The contemporary institutional matrix of journalism is unprepared to either reject objectivity as epistemology or construct something new in its place. Constructing something new would require reasoned, public discourse and that would open the institution up to an unpredictable process of change. Simply rejecting objectivity as an epistemology would require doing without any support for authority. What, then, would be the basis of institutional legitimacy? How could the press claim to "know" and to "report"? In such a case, the epistemology must become implicit. Authority, facticity, and so on must be supported by the latent functions of convention, that is, by ritual form.

Phillips (1972) has presented the practical advantages of objectivity. As encoded in journalistic work procedures, objectivity is a way of efficiently doing one's work. Those work routines result in writing that is seldom controversial, that can be produced quickly and easily without the journalist needing to be an expert on the topic at hand or take responsibility for anything other than who said what, when, and where. For example, journalists can objectively report that a president said such and so about the economy yesterday without needing to establish that those were truthful statements and without needing to understand economic theory.

Tuchman (1972, 1978) demonstrates the ways in which the work procedures that produce what is called objective reporting are also social means for the journalists to manage uncertainty and reduce risk. They are essentially ritual forms that divide the world into known and unknown, safe and unsafe, and manage contacts between the regions. In this they function in the manner of rituals, symbols, and cognitive categories of purity and danger (Douglas, 1966/1978).

If the work procedures of objectivity are, in some aspect at least, ritual forms protecting a community from contact with the unknown and dangerous, and simultaneously embodying their founding concepts, world-view, and the basis of their public legitimacy, then we should expect them to be treated as sacred. Any threat to them will receive an out-of-proportion defensive response. Eason's (1988) examination of the Janet Cooke scandal—responses to revelations that Cooke's Pulitzer Prize winning news stories included various fictional devices, including the invention of their major character—shows exactly that. Eason discusses a number of internal forces that for some time have been moving the institution of journalism away from naive dependence on "objectivity" and toward something new. These include the rise of new journalism and of narrative techniques, of investigative reporting, the use of anonymous sources, of sources without institutional legitimacy, and the general awareness that objectivity is based on a weak philosophy.

Despite this movement, when it was reported that Cooke's stories did not conform to conventional objective news reporting techniques, it became a scandal that was a public embarrassment. In responding to that embarrassment, most journalists forgot that they themselves had questions about the idea and practice of objectivity, that they knew the line between fact and fiction was difficult to draw, and worst of all, that the Janet Cooke situation was probably produced by their own institutional practices and was not a solo-authored work of Ms. Cooke. Rather than rational reflection, what resulted was ritual expulsion. Rather than the norms and procedures of journalistic investigation and writing, what was questioned were the hiring, promotion, and management procedures that put Ms. Cooke where she was. Ms. Cooke became a symbol of the community's vulnerabilities; as she was expelled, the community was ritually strengthened. Just as the punishment for crime has the function of reinforcing the moral order and community boundaries, the expulsion of Janet Cooke functioned to reinforce the codes of journalism and purify the profession. These functions were achieved even as, on the surface, the scandal served as an opportunity to debate the very codes of convention and authority they maintained.

The role of ritual and myth in news work can be seen in the construction of careers as well as their destruction. Zelizer (1990, 1992) shows how narratives in the form of autobiographical history support journalistic authority. Discussion of the Kennedy assassination by news personnel, for example, beginning in the first few days and accelerating later in retrospective reports and in journalists' biographies, is structured by references to where the journalists were and what they witnessed. The conclusions of these stories, though, are claims to authority: "I was there then" is transformed into "You can trust me now." This is a symbolic transformation that works at the level of text by the logic of narrative. It is also a symbolic transformation working at the level of social relations by the logic of myth and ritual: The journalist's first-person narrative about the past is the motivation for the sign of the journalist's authority in third-person accounts about what happened today. Those present then become—magically, mythically, ritually—those who know now.

Elliott (1982) discusses several forms of journalistic behavior that can be seen as ritualistic responses to certain forms of public behavior, portrayed in the forms of media coverage as threats to the social order. Ettema (1990) provides a sensitive analysis of the ritual structures in the relations among press coverage, mayoral politics, and race relations in what was called the Cokely affair in Chicago. Many other examples could be given.

To know what to respond to, and to respond, to coordinate activities with others, to produce a cultural artifact—the news story—that will be received in an understanding way by an already constituted audience, the journalist's work must be ordered by shared symbolic conventions. In this, journalists are like any other cultural workers (see H. S. Becker, 1982). Given the institutional centrality of journalism and the public nature of their work, the use of those symbolic conventions becomes a tricky business. If a painter deviates from the conventions of a genre, he or she may be engaged in artistic experimentation with results that may or may not be aesthetically successful. When journalists deviate from the conventions of their genre, the results are treated as worthy of suspicion. Journalistic writing to convention is a social activity, following symbolic convention, for participation in the serious life, and is backed up by moral authority, in other words, it is a ritualized activity.

If journalistic writing to convention functions as a ritualized activity, then we should expect it to have various ritual powers—of conservation, integration, and transformation, for example. Thus the rituals of news work are not just matters of how journalists do their work, but of how the "events" they "cover" are ritually transformed into stories of appropriate form, and of how audience members are ritually invited into symbolic participation.

8.4

Television as Religion

Gerbner and his associates on the Cultural Indicators Projects have claimed that television is a modern religion: "Television provides, perhaps for the first time since preindustrial religion, a strong cultural link, a shared daily ritual of highly compelling and informative content, between the elites and all other publics" (Gerbner, Gross, Morgan, & Signorielli, 1982, p. 102; cf. Marsden, 1980). It is sometimes difficult to know how literally the Cultural Indicators group wishes to be taken in this claim, especially as they also claim most television watching is merely habitual. They could be trying to provoke a few insights by use of metaphor, or they could be claiming much more sweepingly that television—the viewing, the programs, the institution—really is a religious phenomenon. They devote little attention to the details of ritual and religious studies to help readers discern their seriousness about this claim; their primary concern is usually with more specific claims deriving from their research on television content and viewers. The implicit social theory of their work is essentially British structural-functionalism but with a critical attitude (see esp. Gerbner & Gross, 1976, pp. 173-179):

> The heart of the analogy of television and religion, and the similarity of their social functions, lies in the continual repetition of patterns (myths, ideologies, 'facts,' relationships, etc.), which serve to define the world and legitimize the social order. (Gerbner, Gross, Morgan, & Signorielli, 1986, p. 18)

There are three important points about the study of television and its audience that Gerbner and his associates derive from their implicit anthropological theory. First, the most important effects of television are not short-term dramatic changes but long-term stabilities. Second, more common and more important than attitudes or behaviors that result from persuasion are "facts" and "knowledge" that result from symbolic experience. In symbolic performance, television implicitly defines and informs, analogous to a cognitive effect of ritual (see Lukes, 1975). Third, if television is a storyteller, then meanings are central. Focusing on meaning subtly but decisively redefines the issues for a communication effects researcher. Concern is no longer just for children who may imitate the violence they see on television (analogous to a persuasion or a learning effect), it is for all viewers for whom the meanings of the portrayed violence may lead to fear, alienation, resentment, or misplaced trust. (But note that their conventional social science methods are not well adapted to the study of meanings, as Newcomb, 1978, has pointed out.)

If the Gerbner group were interested in a whole complement of studies that would place television and other media within an anthropological understanding of modern societies, they would also have addressed other issues. They present their theory mostly as a set of assumptions or blanket claims, without supporting evidence or argument. In summaries of their work by others, isolated statements invite caricature. Most critics have attacked their methods, interpretations of their data, or the evidence supporting specific conclusions (e.g., Doob & MacDonald, 1979; Hirsch, 1980). A more detailed knowledge of the anthropological litera- ture reinforces the claim that the institution of television is a religious phenome- non with more seriousness—though it remains incompletely investigated.

Goethals (1981, 1985) also pursues the idea that television watching is reli- gious, but from another angle, giving attention primarily to forms of television content comparable to aspects of the Judeo-Christian tradition. The book is mostly illustration, not pushing the argument through to conclusion at either a theoretical or empirical level, but it is informed illustration, demonstrating that television uses symbolic forms that preceded it in religious traditions.

Goethals's argument has three bases of support. Television participates in ritual and presents various things ritualistically; television participates in the presentation and interpretation of icons; television is also one of our main sources of iconoclasm (the more aggressive form of religious maintenance and renewal, historically characteristic of Protestant cultures and currently important in revivals of Muslim fundamentalism, for example). Ritual appears in special events; the icons appear mostly in drama and some in news, but they are crys- talized in their most perfect form in advertising; iconoclasm appears on news, documentaries, and talk shows.

Television presents both traditional and new rituals, creating for its viewers some of the feeling of presence in the ritual space (cf. Dayan & Katz, 1992). Goethals points out that traditional ritual creates its own space and time, "trans- porting" the faithful out of the daily round and into contact with the transcendent, the holy, the territory of ultimate meaning. The difference that makes a difference in such cases is not between those who are there and those who are not but between those who are faithful and those who are not (cf. Dayan, Katz, & Kerns, 1984). (Goethals seems to have been startled into taking media events seriously by Pope John Paul II blessing the television viewers over the airwaves.) Tele- vision coverage of politics, Goethals claims, is adopting more of these ritual forms, perhaps transforming that supposedly secular realm into a religious realm, at least as experienced on TV. This idea deserves investigation.

By way of a useful afterword in the final chapter, Goethals (1981) points out that television both solemnizes and trivializes, that the faithful both are (sym- bolically) and are not (physically) transported into participation by the television presentation of ritual. They do not get wet if it rains, but they do get blessed if the Pope says so.

9

Ritual Functions
of Mediated Culture

Claims by Goethals and by Gerbner and his colleagues that television is a religion, discussed in the last chapter, depend on the claim that much of television content serves ritual functions. Many other scholars have also pointed to certain ritual functions of television content, and other areas of popular culture, but without it being part of that larger, less likely claim. That literature on media content and popular culture needs to be reviewed separately.

Partially, we are shifting attention from media form to media content, analogous to a shift from ritual to myth. The literature on myth, and related concepts, in media content and popular culture is large and heterogeneous. Though obviously the ideas are importantly related, most of the literature on myth does not depend explicitly on a concept of ritual. Most of it, also, is concerned primarily with structures of text and artifact as such. Contrasting with this, our purpose is to examine the role of those texts in ritual. In order to keep the discussion from being pulled into the large literature on myth, and losing its focus on ritual, our emphasis will be on ritual *functions* of media content, rather than on media content and popular culture per se. The logic is that no matter how mythic in structure, a text or artifact is not an element of ritual until it is put to use by people and functions in that way.

These studies fall into three areas: myth and ritual, moral dramas, and modeling of social roles.

9.1

News, Television, and
Popular Culture as Myth and Ritual

One version of myth analysis applied to the media and popular culture in industrial societies was discussed, and criticized, in section 3.5. In that approach, myth in capitalist societies was identified as ideology, and ideology was cast as a form of lying. Another version of myth analysis, known as the myth and symbol school, common among an earlier generation of U.S. scholars, was characteristically more optimistic (e.g., Slote, 1963; H. N. Smith, 1950). Syntheses of these and other perspectives, especially the work of Lévi-Strauss (e.g., 1958/1963, 1962/1966, 1964/1970), have proved useful in the analysis of television drama, news, and commercials. There is a large literature in this area, but here we will discuss only a few examples in which the connection of myth and ritual is explicit.

In characterizing television or other media as mythic, they are identified as instances of the central symbol systems of the society at hand, and therefore worthy of the careful treatment anthropologists accord the myth, ritual, and central symbol systems of the cultures they study. Silverstone (1988) has identified three distinct supports for such a claim.

First, "television presents the content of myth, most significantly in its reporting of major collectively focused and focusing events, like coronations, weddings, or ball games" (Silverstone, 1988, p. 29). This applies not only to special events but also to ordinary news and ordinary entertainment programs that are mythically structured and populated with mythic types. As Bird and Dardenne (1988, p. 71) put it, "News stories, like myth, do not tell it like it is, but rather tell it like it means." Over and over again, the U.S. media present stories of good versus evil, us versus them, civilization versus chaos, the enduring importance of kinship, claims to primordiality, Christian themes, variations on Oedipus, Horatio Alger, freedom, manifest destiny, and so on. Soap operas provide many examples:

> As the stable small town fades, the soap opera keeps alive its idealized replica, the image of a community in which everyone knows or is related to everyone else, where continuity counts more than transience, where right and wrong are unambiguous, where good triumphs over evil. It is a world dominated by the domestic values of the family. (Rosen, 1986, p. 49)

The presentation of mythic content and mythic form is not limited to special events; it is typical of news, entertainment programming and, as Goethals (1981) and Goffman (1976) point out, especially advertising. Moments of social crisis, disorder, or disruption may increase the prevalence, and presumably also the utility, of myth and its ritual functions in media content. Hallin and Gitlin (1993) found a large component of ritual and civil religion in U.S. television journalists' coverage of the Gulf War.

Overlapping with the first point is Silverstone's (1988) second, that television

> presents a communication, which in its various narrative and rhetorical aspects preserves forms of familiar and formulaic story-telling that are the product and property of a significantly oral culture. (p. 29)

The idea that the form of much of television content is mythic, that story structures are few, familiar, and inherited, is not controversial and could be seen as part of the first point. However, Silverstone is also affirming a point made in various ways, sometimes controversially, by McLuhan and a few others (e.g., Meyrowitz, 1985), that as a form of communication, television depends on conventions and has typical effects distinct from those of print-literate culture, and that these other conventions appear to share characteristics with "pre-literate" or oral cultures (see useful analyses of these ideas in Carey, 1969, 1981; Gronbeck, 1981, 1991).

The third point is even more questionable, and provocative. This point proposes that television

> creates by its technology a distinct spatial and temporal environment marked by the screen and marking for all to see the tissue boundary between the profane and the sacred. (Silverstone, 1988, p. 29)

Silverstone argues that there is something premodern, essentially magical, about television and its social status. Newcomb and Hirsch (1984) have also claimed that television has the liminal quality of ritual; something about the conjunction of the TV set, the institution, and the audience viewing constitutes a modern, secular ritual. St. Clair Harvey (1990) makes a similar, though more particular, claim, arguing that music videos have a distinctly magical, symbolic power. Hoover (1988) makes such a claim in regard to the special case of the audience for religious broadcasting. The point is that watching television draws viewers into another experience, one that is not wholly here and now, one that is not wholly fact or fiction, reality or fantasy. One could argue that television shares this with other forms of communication, but since television is such a dominating medium for most people it may be worth while distinguishing it. One implication is that the television viewing experience requires anthropological study (Sáenz, 1992).

Myth is a basic human form of expression. Myth gives voice to, and thus makes public, deep anxieties as well as basic beliefs and values. "Despite their manifest implausibilities, [myths] are coherent and logical and represent, above all, a culture thinking about itself" (Silverstone, 1988, p. 29, discussing Lévi-Strauss's contributions). Myth, like ritual, has several important connections with reality usually not credited by critics subscribing to the myth = ideology = lying school of thought. It is a form for expressing, thereby sharing, and thereby creating the conditions for the resolution of socially originating but personally experienced anxieties. Certain problems become the subject of myth because they are common problems.

Myth is a way of holding a society and its people up to the standards they profess. The Watergate scandal took on mythic form because it was, in part, an argument about which interpretations of basic American ideas would rule the actions of the individuals running the U.S. government (J. C. Alexander, 1984, 1988a). The ideas celebrated by inaugurations and other state and political events, commemorations, and religious ceremonies do not have unalloyed control over their participants' daily lives, but they are a model of a better world, and their periodic celebration draws attention to the possibilities.

Finally, myth is a way of managing social change. Though we do not usually think of myth or ritual as things that can be questioned—they have more the design of answers or of submission than questions or challenges—still, they are means by which fundamental issues are brought into discourse, and thus made available to debate. In point of fact, liturgies and their interpretations are constantly in process of change, as the history of any church shows. The "timelessness" of myth and ritual is a part of the experience of ritual but not a part of its history.

9.2

Moral Dramas

Sutherland and Siniawsky (1982) found that soap opera characters violating moral standards (deceit, murder, illicit sex) were later punished in the story three times more often than they were allowed to get away with it. Though the authors do not provide a ritual interpretation of this observation, it is clear how one would work. As Durkheim (1895/1982) pointed out, even crime has a positive social function. In being labeled as crime and being punished, it dramatizes moral standards. Crime and punishment are symbols that bring abstract ideas of social order into everyday practice. Soap operas perform the same function. Rosen (1986) points out that soap operas function as morality plays that never end. Though the stories are dominated by domestic values, the plot tensions are produced by potential eruptions in that system of control. As each plot thread comes to an end, violating characters are brought back into the symbolic community/family through dramatic portrayals of punishment, regret, forgiveness, and redemption. Burke (e.g., 1966, 1989) has also provided sensitive analyses of the moral-ritual functions of the dramas of life and art.

As Stevens (1985) points out, just as morals are not closed and unchanging systems, so dramas about them are not completely scripted. Reinforcement is only one of the possible outcomes of the negotiation of moral boundaries. We should expect the media to devote the most attention to morals when the morals themselves are being questioned or during periods of social and cultural change. His analysis of newspaper coverage of sensational murder and divorce trials in 1920s America provides support for this hypothesis.

From this point of view, it is worth noting that "much of the earliest news-reporting took the form of Puritan-inspired pamphlets relating accidents and disasters of moral importance" (Thomas, 1971, p. 96). If U.S. news reporting began with an interest in showing the "hand of God in daily events" (p. 93)—the first U.S. newspaper in 1690 promised to print "memorable occurrents of Divine Providence"—then it should be no surprise that latent moral functions exist in the news today.

9.3

Modeling of Social Roles

The phenomenon of the media star is usually understood in terms of the star system, a business practice. Stars are understood as decision-making and business-planning efficiencies, products of institutional structures and processes, reifications of the logic of commodity relations (e.g., Buxton, 1990; deCordova, 1990). But as J. L. Reeves (1988) points out, this cannot be all they are. Stars must also be operating at the levels of the logic of symbols and the interpretation of meanings. Stars must be understood as both commodity and communication.

J. L. Reeves (1988) borrows a typology of stars from Dyer (1979): Stars are differentiated from the bulk of other performers by virtue of taking some ordinary social type to its extreme (Marilyn Monroe, Sylvester Stallone), putting a unique inflection on some basic, probably iconic social type (detectives, cowboys, good bad girls), or by being so artfully various that they resist typification (Madonna). Reeves posits an intriguing idea about how this works. Borrowing a general idea of the ritual functions of communication from Carey (see sec. 12.2) and specific ideas about how language works from Bakhtin, he proposes that "star-audience identification . . . involves a ritual interplay between living social relations at work in the commonsense world and the mediated human representations of those relations" (p. 150). Stars' characters represent familiar types, pushed to extremes, performed uniquely, or intriguingly mixed with other. In one way or another

> the star makes the typical strange, the ordinary extraordinary. And in making the typical strange, the star . . . allows us access to our 'own language as it is perceived in someone else's language' [quoting Bakhtin].
>
> In this scheme, stardom as media discourse becomes the individualized articulation of relevant, strategic social types that represent culturally significant ways of speaking, or seeing, or being. (J. L. Reeves, 1988, p. 153)

The star is a symbol of a social type, a ritual performance of an otherwise ordinary way of being (cf. Goethals, 1981).

A more detailed assessment, though of narrower range than Reeves, is Goffman's (1976) *Gender Advertisements*. The body of the book (pp. 28-83) is devoted to the stereotypic forms of gender display evident in (mostly) magazine advertising photographs. This is informed, first, by a delineation of the ritual order as a structure of all social interaction (pp. 1-9; see also Collins, 1986; Goffman, 1959, 1967, 1983b; Rawls, 1987; and sec. 11.1) and second, by a painstaking analysis (a) of the nature of pictorial and especially photographic representation, (b) of the possible relations between pictures and social realities, (c) of the possible forms of participation of pictures in social processes, and (d) of the epistemological and methodological status of photographs (pp. 10-27). Goffman's conclusion is that much of advertising and media content consists of hyperritualizations. The genre of commercial realism is built on the extra-careful display of already narrowly structured display forms.

It is not a point that Goffman chooses to drive home, but his work invites the reader, and especially those concerned with the social functions of the media, to conclude that the hyperritualized displays of advertising also function in the maintenance of larger social orders. The ritual displays of advertising are hyper in more than one sense (going beyond Goffman's explicit claims): they are more carefully constructed and more stereotypical in form than displays in ordinary life and, in addition to appearing as records of alignments in actual social situations, advertising photographs function as alignment displays themselves. At that second level, the alignment displayed is not one of a person in an ongoing social situation—that would not normally include the reader or audience member—but of an image in a larger order of signs, rhetorics, and interpretations that does include the reader. At that level, the "backward" reference of the ritual is not to a social or cosmic order in which the people displayed in the photograph are positioned but to an order of social meanings in which the reader is invited to place his or her own self. The profusion of hyperritualized gender displays in advertising and other media content both narrows the distribution of socially available models and lends an authority to a few, often-repeated models.

The reference to the serious life may not be as clear here as it is in the case of media events. By some lights, the displays of image and style in the media are purely secular affairs. Others, however, find them profane, issues of grave seriousness. Goffman's (1976) modeling analysis identifies continuities between the worlds of interpersonal and media symbolics. They are together ritual mechanisms for the construction of a social world in which certain images are valued, certain ways of being empowered.

One evening as I sat on the front porch, I observed two early-teen girls walking by. They were laughing about the stylized, sashaying walk of female fashion models. "Oh sure, I could never walk that way," one said, incredulously, while executing a caricatured imitation. It was clear that, though their words were mocking the fashion advertising standard, their body movements were practicing it.

The patter of DJs between songs does not just express what they are saying but models a way of being in the world. It has the iconic function that Goethals discusses; it is a hyperritualization, in Goffman's terms. As Reeves points out, identification with a media character is not a simple attraction phenomenon. Rather, by listening to a favorite DJ, fans are orienting themselves to a ritual display of orientation in a world of sounds and meanings.

10

Political, Rhetorical, and Civic Rituals

Political and civic ceremonies, and the public speaking associated with them, constitute distinct social forms. Though these days in the U.S. almost all political events attract media coverage—and, as K. Becker (1995) points out, that coverage is often an important element of a process of ritualization—they still depend crucially on in-person dynamics. Locations have to be set up, crowds gathered, events conducted. Much of this work is to produce ritual form, almost all of it serves ritual functions.

10.1

The Symbolics of State and Power;
Rituals of Political Oratory and Ceremony;
Elections and Politics as Ritual

The effectivity of symbols in ritual, and the gravity of the realities they constitute, has been most clearly demonstrated in studies of political ritual. One of the books that helped establish the principle that anthropological theory developed for the study of ritual and religion was also appropriate to the study of politics, was Geertz's (1980) *Negara,* a study of what he called the theater state of Bali.

Bali, especially as it appears in the 19th century documents examined by Geertz, was a fabulously ritualized place. The state system was exceedingly hierarchial, every bit of it expressed in ritual form—including clothing and personal

ornament, architecture, statuary and other art forms, rules of deference and demeanor, inheritance, parades, processions, and ceremonies of great variety. Central to the affairs of state were huge ceremonies, some requiring months of preparation and involving tens of thousands of people. These ceremonies, along with
many of the other ritual forms, took on dramatic forms that could be read nar-
ratively to at once express and enact the hierarchies of the state.

> The state ceremonies of classical Bali were metaphysical theatre: theatre de-
> signed to express a view of the ultimate nature of reality and, at the same time,
> to shape the existing conditions of life to be consonant with that reality; that is,
> theatre to present an ontology and, by presenting it, to make it happen—make it
> actual. (Geertz, 1980, p. 104)

No progress can be made in understanding such a social order with a preju-
dice "that 'symbolic' opposes to 'real' as fanciful to sober, figurative to literal,
obscure to plain, aesthetic to practical, mystical to mundane, and decorative to
substantial" (p. 136). That mode of thinking must be set aside, "along with the
allied one that the dramaturgy of power is external to its workings" (p. 136). In
this situation the dramaturgy of power *was* its working; "the state drew its force,
which was real enough, from its imaginative energies, its semiotic capacity to make
inequality enchant" (p. 123). As Goffman (1976) said in a different context,

> the expression of subordination and domination through this swarm of situ-
> ational means is more than a mere tracing or symbol or ritualistic affirmation of
> the social hierarchy. These expressions considerably constitute the hierarchy;
> they are the shadow *and* the substance. (p. 6)

But it is easy, in the comfort of a reading chair, to treat classical Bali as a
spectacle. My, what a wonderfully different place it was; whatever Geertz relates
about it is probably true enough—fascinating reading, certainly. But the general
conclusion, the lesson of the study is of a different order.

> Ideas are not . . . unobservable mental stuff. They are envehicled meanings, the
> vehicles being symbols (or in some usages, signs), a symbol being anything that
> denotes, describes, represents, exemplifies, labels, indicates, evokes, depicts,
> expresses—anything that somehow or other signifies. And anything that some-
> how or other signifies is intersubjective, thus public, thus accessible to overt and
> corrigible *plein air* explication. Arguments, melodies, formulas, maps, and pic-
> tures are not idealities to be stared at but texts to be read; so are rituals, palaces,
> technologies, and social formations. (Geertz, 1980, p. 135)

The reading of a text is a form of action that brings about some of what it expresses. The same is true in all societies everywhere:

> At the political center of any complexly organized society . . . there is both a governing elite and a set of symbolic forms expressing the fact that it is in truth governing. No matter how democratically the members of the elite are chosen . . . or how deeply divided among themselves they may be . . . they justify their existence and order their actions in terms of a collection of stories, ceremonies, insignia, formalities, and appurtenances that they have either inherited or, in more revolutionary situations, invented. It is these—crowns and coronations, limousines and conferences—that mark the center as center and give what goes on there its aura of being not merely important but in some odd fashion connected with the way the world is built. The gravity of high politics and the solemnity of high worship spring from liker impulses than might first appear. (Geertz, 1977, pp. 152-153)

If this is so, then ritual forms should be identifiable within what are otherwise thought of as strictly practical political activities in officially secular societies. Indeed, such work is common (B. Alexander, 1987; J. C. Alexander, 1988b; Gusfield & Michalowicz, 1984). Lane (1981) provides an extended analysis of Soviet political ritual; van Bremen and Martinez (1995) provide examples from contemporary Japan. The anthologies of Bak (1990), Cannadine and Price (1987), and Wilentz (1985) provide a variety of historical examples, mostly from Europe and Asia. Cooper and Worden (1989) provide a comparative study of the development of national symbols and rituals in newly independent nations following World War II; Zei (1995) provides a historical study of the changes of national symbols and rituals in Slovenia across the 20th century. Here we will focus briefly on U.S. political ritual.

Bennett (1977) points out that in addition to the pragmatic or strategic conditions on the construction of political oratory that we usually take into account, there are also ritualistic constraints. Political speeches include certain features for ritual, as well as strategic, purposes. Under political pressures, certain genres of rhetoric may be more constrained by ritual structures than others—apologia for example (Gold, 1978). Similarly, certain types of political event or process conventionally require more ritual form than others. Gronbeck (1978b) uses ritual concepts to analyse processes of political corruption and rectification, for example; Gronbeck (1978a) has also applied the ritual frame to the political campaign process. Trent (1978) has pointed out that certain first acts of a campaign have a ritual power. Among the activities of the campaign, the party conventions are one of the most clearly ritualistic ceremonies (Farrell, 1978).

Most of these studies identify ritual forms *within* the political; others analyze the whole of the political *as* ritual. This depends on the ontological claim that human action is symbolic just as the symbolic is a form of action.

Sometimes special events impress observers with their ceremony, emphasis on performance, and attention to narrative and ritual structures, such as in J. C. Alexander's (1984, 1988a) analyses of the Watergate crisis period as a large, dispersed ritualistic process. The social drama unfolding around the kidnapping and subsequent assassination of leading Italian politician Aldo Moro by the Red Brigades in 1978 is another example. As Wagner-Pacifici (1986) demonstrates, the event was the centerpiece of a social drama of ritualistic competition, conflict, and crisis, involving the state, the political parties, the Catholic Church, Red Brigades, students, media, Moro's family, and other citizens. She rejects "ritual" as a label for the whole drama, emphasizing the competition between parties and ideas to dominate the symbolization and interpretation of the events, which resulted in no one conceptualization of events in the form of *a* ritual. Nevertheless, the logic of ritual—in the expansive sense in which we are using the term—structured the activities of the competing parties and provided structures for representations of their ideas.

The logic of ritual analysis needs to be turned on routine political events as well. Baker (1983), among others (Marvin, 1994; McGerr, 1986; McLeod, 1993; Schudson, 1994), has proposed that we seek to understand political processes by reading them, treating them as text and ritual; that is, as activities with primarily expressive value.

> From this perspective election campaigns become community rituals embodying national values, what Victor Turner calls 'a storage unit' into which, over the years, Americans placed information about their political norms, beliefs, sentiments, and roles. As ritual, election campaigns summarize political customs, traditions, and designs, and within this ritual, voting, the master symbol, encompasses a series of public meanings. . . . Such an approach to political history explores the latent function, not the purposive goals of selecting a president and vice-president. . . .
>
> The issue is not what choices presidential elections offered voters. . . . Concern shifts to other matters: Where and how did Americans vote? What preparations did they undergo before doing so? What metaphorical language and political iconography did they use? . . . At issue is what public ceremonies reveal about American values. (pp. 262-263)

In the ritual of politics that Baker examines—mid-19th century elections, especially the activities of the Democratic Party in Northern states—it was important that the Democratic Party organize its parades and rallies in military fashion. In this way, the individual was fused with the group; individual will became expressed as a part of the more powerful body of group will.

> The parades in which members became active partisans, enact[ed] the military behaviors of their language. . . . Again the occasion was more expressive than instrumental, more inspirational than informative, and more directed at promoting internal unity than at generating external propaganda. With their well-ordered rows of Democratic marchers, parades reified the essential concept of American political culture—the people's will—by providing a collective activity that unified diverse individuals. (pp. 292-293)

The form of the ritual of voting leveled status differences and reintegrated groups because in that act individuals were individuals. They voted on a first-come first-served basis; each vote counted the same. Polling was organized by geography and not by party affiliation, religion, class, occupation, or other distinctions (for those enfranchised to vote, that is). Note how different this is from the old Soviet system of voting in the factory, with an explicit emphasis on class membership.

> Thus the procedures of American voting diluted the group solidarity built up during the campaign and reduced post-election tensions among partisans. In casting their vote, the people became the sum of its individuals, not of its groups. (pp. 309-310)

Baker continues,

> Never a seismograph of issue-related choice, voting was feeling, instinct, and behavior, and participation in its nineteenth-century rituals was never an act of unrestrained power. Nor was the equality of election day anything more than a temporary condition. But because elections brought Americans together in celebrations that began as a display of difference and ended in consent and the conveyance of power, they provided an adaptive mechanism that proved all the more essential in threatening times. (pp. 315-316)

Schudson (1994) suggests that contemporary voting in the U.S. be understood as a rite, thus an expression of citizenship. Viewed in this way, declining voter participation reflects not apathy so much as the tension between progressive democratic ideals and late 20th century lived experience. Increasing numbers of Americans sensibly opt out of voting because they cannot live up to the ideals they have been taught it is supposed to express.

Marvin (1994; cf. McLeod, 1993) proposes that the act of voting is one part of a larger ritual progression:

> A primary season, a nominating convention, an election, an inauguration: All are set pieces, contrived dramas of sex and death, symbolic disruptions of the family healed, exposed once more to disintegration and healed again, at least for the "honeymoon" following a successful mating. (p. 287)

There is an element of ceremony in even the most practical political activities. There are two important aspects to this. First, the element of ceremony in politics requires that there be some religious logic in this otherwise secular realm (B. Alexander, 1987). Second, politics must, in part, be conducted as ceremonial communication, adapted to ceremonial and communicative as well as political requirements. In varying degrees of explicitness, extending these ideas from politics to all modern life is a theme of the next two chapters.

10.2

Rhetorical Rituals and Ritual Rhetoric

We cannot discuss political communication without reference to speech making, nor speech making without reference to the venerable literature of rhetorical theory. That tradition of theory, though, is a bit at odds with the point of view of ritual studies. Rationalist presumptions run so deeply in rhetorical theory, that ritual and ceremonial have been treated as a separate topic, and the possibility of ritual aspects of rationalist or strategic rhetoric have hardly been considered (cf. Bennett, 1977; Carter, 1991).

Epideictic, defined by Aristotle as "the ceremonial oratory of display," is a classical category of rhetoric (Burgess, 1902/1987). In modern usage, epideictic has come to refer to celebratory or ceremonial rhetoric; eulogies, speeches of introduction, and award ceremony speeches are typical examples. The social functions of epideictic are much the same as those of ritual, and epideictic often is ritualistic (Carter, 1991), but Ochs (1993) warns that the two concepts should not be equated. Surely not all celebratory rhetoric is ritual. Symmetrically, not all rituals would have rhetorical features, but there is an area of important overlap.

Hoban (1980) follows the anthropological and philosophical literature to identify a category of rhetorical occasions and performances that are ritual. Others use rhetorical and ideological theory to identify categories or aspects of ritual that are rhetorical (e.g., Bloch, 1975, 1989).

Ritual rhetoric has several features that distinguish it from other types of rhetoric. In Hoban's analysis, the most important is that, when successful, like Austin's felicitous speech act, it synthesizes subjective and objective experience, individual and communal orientations. Clearly, that is one of the major elements of ritual and probably a key purpose or function of rhetorical ritual. Though it does not appear radically different from Bryant's (1953) nomination of the adjustment of ideas to people and people to ideas as the purpose of all rhetoric, that purpose is achieved differently when rhetoric is used ritually than when it is used argumentatively. To reuse the classic categories, adjustments of people and ideas would be achieved differently in epideictic than in forensic rhetoric.

Hoban identifies four features of rhetorical rituals. In addition to aiming at "an interpenetration of an objective display and a subjective experience" (p. 288), they are both instrumental and "consumatory" performances, meaning they are adapted to goals beyond themselves, in light of which they have the status of means, and they are ends in themselves, valuable for their own sake. In Parsons's (1937/1968) terminology they are both instrumental and normative acts. Third, being liminal and performative phenomena, with an emphasis on aesthetics, the ritual rhetoric differs in form from more conventionally discursive and logical rhetoric. Fourth (though Hoban only mentions it in passing, for our purposes it is worth isolating), the ideas presented in ritual rhetoric are, for the faithful, unquestionable. Hence there is no issue—for at least some of the audience—of probability, reasoning, and persuasion; this clearly gives the rhetorical critic a very different responsibility when evaluating ritual rhetoric, than when evaluating the adaptedness of conventional rhetoric (cf. Grimes, 1990).

Knuf (1994) provides an analysis of ritualized political language in the German Democratic Republic; the ideas are easily generalized to show both the power—and danger—of ritual in political oratory. Certain terms and phrases important to a political ideology—such as freedom, democracy, progress—can come to be used in ritualistic ways. The words then lose their referentiality and take on the performative effectivity of ritual. Proper ritual use of the words, then, constitutes the reality the words refer to; the words can only be evaluated within the ritual use and not by reference to an external reality. But of course, the breakdown of the GDR and the reunification of Germany, like all such cases of social change, reminds us that ritually enforced order can be challenged and changed, even if its symbols do not invite us to do so.

10.3

Public Festivals and Ceremonies

In addition to political processes and events, political communication, and rhetoric, community life is punctuated by a variety of civic celebrations: parades, holidays, anniversaries, reunions, and so on. Ritual is an element of all of these.

Warner's (1959) study of Memorial Day celebrations exemplifies most of the key issues. Warner illustrates how the celebrations served as both symbolic and actual reunions; the syntax of the daylong events began by performing social separations and ended by bringing the members of different social positions together. As Lukes (1975) points out, such community celebrations can have a conflictful edge that is an important part of their meaning (cf. Moore & Myerhoff, 1975, 1977). The collection of case studies edited by Turner (1982a) provides a number of detailed examples. Foley's (1990) study of high school football as ritual is an extended example. Manning (1983) and Browne (1980) offer collections of essays on community festivals, sporting events, carnival, rodeos, and other celebratory ritual forms. Frese (1993) offers studies of ritual and ceremony in a range of American ethnic, geographical, class, and culture groupings, part of the point of the anthology being that civic ceremonies function to maintain and celebrate American cultural diversity. Johnston (1991) discusses the apparent proliferation of anniversary celebrations in Europe and America in the 1980s—such things as the bicentennial of the constitution, tricentennial of Philadelphia, bicentennial of Mozart's death, and the bicentennial of the French Revolution (cf. Gillis, 1994). Clearly such events mark the passage of time, as well as some form of relation with the past—though it may be one of distance and difference. Johnston argues that they are proliferating and that that indicates a growing concern with the passage of historical time, probably tied to a nascent notion of the significance of the approaching millennium.

Most students of civic ceremonies have had a primary interest in either the events as such or in analysis of their social functions. Handelman (1990) offers one of the few attempts at a general theoretical account (see also Chaney, 1993, for an approach emphasizing drama and spectacle rather than ritual and ceremony). An implication of his work that he chooses not to analyze formally is that such events can have social functions only via their communicative capacities. The same implication is clear across the case studies and essays collected in Turner (1982a), and such was argued for the general case of ritual in Chapter 6 of this book. What is needed, then, are studies of civil ceremonies by students of communication, who are equipped to analyze their specific communicative devices.

11

Ritual Communication Forms in Everyday Secular Life

In this chapter, we turn attention to the ritual aspects of everyday, ordinary, secular activities. Some of the discussion of mediated communication in Chapters 8 and 9 also addressed the ordinary and daily. Here attention is given primarily to face-to-face activities.

The first and longest section of the chapter is devoted to the work of Goffman and other scholars who have analyzed the ritual elements of interpersonal interaction. This work deserves lengthy discussion because it provides a model on which so many other applications of ritual concepts are based. The second section addresses the issue of style. Though obviously style is a part of interpersonal ritual, it is also a distinct topic because of its relation to the fashion and popular culture industries. Style has also been treated as an important topic in communication studies because of its function in identifying membership in social categories, such as class, race, gender, sexual orientation, subcultures, and leisure and interest groups. The final section addresses rituals of organizational and work life.

11.1

Interpersonal and Microsocial Rituals

When two bicyclists crash into each other in the park, to build on Weber's (1922/1978, pp. 375 ff.) example, they are engaged in simple behavior. Presumably it could be adequately explained by reference to physical causes. When they pick themselves up off the ground and begin to shout at each other, they are engaged in social action. Their behavior is action because its causes include motive, reason, and meaning as well as physical-organic phenomena; it is social action because it is meaningfully oriented to others.

There is need in human society for unambiguous signs of the nature of social encounters. One of the bicyclists may have looked contrite, said "I'm sorry," and hurried to help the other up; one or both may have furrowed their brows, tightened their lips and other face muscles, formed a fist, pulled an arm and a shoulder back, mumbled obscenities, and begun a deliberate walk toward the other. In either case, and other possibilities, there are elements of performance mixed with the action, there are things said and done simply, and there are things said and done according to form. Generally, in any social encounter, there are matters that are relatively more formally coded and that function as relatively unambiguous signs as to who people are, what their intentions are, who they think the other is, what they expect the other to do, what type of encounter they expect, and so on. These are bits of information that co-interactants need in order to manage their participation. The information is encoded in the structure or form of interaction, and these signs provide mostly structural information—who and how more than what and why. Though much more complex and variable, these formally coded behaviors are analogous to the display behavior that ethologists study (e.g., Huxley, 1966a; see sec. 4.1). These bits of formal behavior functioning as signs are present as a ritual element of all social interactions, marking the transition from mere-behavior in the presence of others, to social relation:

> Encounter of a physical kind may take place without such social relationship—as by two persons rubbing shoulders in a bus. They recognize the physical presence of each other but the encounter is not socially acceptable, the existence of each is not incorporated into the social universe of the other. A social relationship is then created only by some exchange of signs, as by a word or a nod. (Firth, 1972, p. 1)

The small ritual forms of nodding, smiling, and saying hello indicate to others in one's environment that they are not just objects but are recognized as members of an order of social relations; a pattern of mutual orientation has been established. The status of person-in-social-relation is independent of the material of the situation, for it is only constructed by the exchange of signs between some of the bodies in any given situation.

Note that it is not necessary to identify all such communication forms as ritual to understand them. Doing so is an analytic option. It draws our attention to their function of constituting social relations, and categorizes them with more elaborately ceremonial forms of communication with more clearly serious consequences—as some of the examples below address.

Once established, social relations can transcend any particular situation and continue to exist relatively independent of space and time; however, they need to be symbolically maintained. Therefore, along with ritual forms of greeting there are ritual forms of parting:

> Forms of greeting and parting are symbolic devices . . . of incorporation or continuance of persons in a social scheme. . . . The informational or emotional content of [such] sign[s] may be highly variable, even minimal. What is of prime relevance is the establishment or perpetuation of a social relationship, the recognition of the other person as a social entity, a personal element in a common social situation. (Firth, 1972, pp. 1-2)

Commonly, when people ask one another "How are you today?" the answer is something to the effect of "fine, how are you?" More elaborate, informative, and honest answers are usually not desired, because information is not the purpose of the conversation. Malinowski (1923/1949, pp. 313-316) designated such speech forms *phatic communion* and the idea has become well known. It is mostly used disparagingly to describe "talk [that] is analyzed to be referentially deficient and communicatively insignificant" (Coupland, Coupland, & Robinson, 1992, p. 209). Actually, E. Goody (1972) shows in detail that much more is being accomplished in such communication forms. These are not silly bits of noninformative, only-apparent communication, they are crucial social rituals that signify and, at least partly, constitute the relation. Coupland, Coupland, and Robinson (1992) also demonstrate the essential social work that is accomplished in phatic communion.

These same phenomena show up in larger ways in both intimate relations and in organizations. Though it is not sufficient, in the United States today, an intimate relation is thought to require a large degree of physical closeness and time spent together. Hence, time spent apart can be experienced as a threat to the relation—at least, that is, unless there are other communicative forms to accommodate the loss of coincidence in time and space. In similar ways, organizations are defined by memberships that appear to have no guarantee when individuals are not co-present. Sigman (1991) has explored these problems of relationships and organizations, showing how they are addressed by time-binding and space-binding communication (see also Knuf, 1989-90, on ritual communication and organizational boundary management).

Sigman (1991) shows how key examples of communication in relationships and organizations work to perform and indicate the continuance of relation across a period of separation, to a greater extent than they offer immediately useful information. As couples prepare to separate for a day of work, they talk about what they will do while they are apart, when they will be back, and what they will do then. Often this will be exactly the same every day: "Bye, honey, have a good day. I'll see you at 5:30." When they get back together again, they talk about where they have been and what they have been doing. Periods of longer separation such as a trip are marked by communicative forms appropriate to the length of separation: phone calls, "I miss you, I love you," sending post-cards, buying souvenirs.

These simple greeting and parting forms are examples of ritual communication that correspond to an element of social order (the relationship), not just because they are an expression of it but because they are a performance of it. The same thing can be traced in more complex examples. Families develop a variety of ritual forms for enacting their relationship and protecting it from the threats of time and geography (e.g., Bossard & Boll, 1950; Haines, 1988; Reiss, 1981; Rosenthal & Marshall, 1988; Wolin & Bennett, 1984). Christmas celebrations in many countries are structured by sets of implicit rules that define ritual orders (Miller, 1993). Caplow and his colleagues (Caplow, 1984; Caplow, Bahr, Chadwick, Hill, & Williamson, 1983, pp. 224-243) have shown that in the United States behavioral choices such as buying a Christmas tree or not, buying a real one or an artificial one, a big one or a little one, sending a card or not and to whom, who buys gifts for whom, of what value, which gifts have to be wrapped and between whom is gift-wrapping optional, from whom and to whom is money given, who travels to whose house and how far, who cooks dinner and what is served—all such behaviors that constitute the U.S. Christmas festivity are extraordinarily patterned, as if governed by rules that everyone knows, though probably few could state. Even more interesting, the rules map onto kinship and social relation structures, so that what matters for these various decisions is who has kids and how many, what their ages are, who has been friends for how long, if the relation is romantic, and so on. The gift giving, Christmas tree buying, dinner preparing, travelling, and so on, in addition to just being the actions they are, at a formal level are also ritually communicative forms for performing family and friendship relations.

Everyday life is at least as complex as we move from one social role to another, from one organization to another, one setting to another. Ritual is a powerful device for the ordinary orderliness people make of the complex variety of everyday social life. Despite our experience, analysis shows there is no unitary self; everyone is an amalgam of partial, ill-defined, overlapping, contradicting, simultaneous, and distinct roles. There is no unitary social world; situations are mixtures of responsibilities, desires, knowledge, relevancies, constraints, re-sources, and performances. In any given moment, one may be polite, attractive, assertive, attentive at some level, unavailable at others, a friend, and a profes-sional; with the choice of a few words, the turn of a conversation, the whole combination shifts like the bits of glass in a kaleidoscope into an utterly new but equally structured pattern. The greatness of Goffman's work is in elucidating the devices by which we manage this mess, by which we fold these multiplexities back into a more or less seamlessly experienced reality. These devices are ritual.

Goffman was explicit about ritual in only some of his work, especially the earlier (esp. 1959, 1967; see also 1963a, 1963b, 1971). But Collins (1986, 1988b) argues convincingly that there is a theoretical continuity to the whole of his work around this issue (see also Drew & Wooton, 1988; Giddens, 1988; Strong, 1988). Goffman's later work (e.g., 1974, 1981, 1983a, 1983b) offers more sophisticated versions of many of his earlier ideas, though sometimes in a new vocabulary.

In the early work, Goffman presents people as performers, required by their situations to put forth particular lines of interaction in particular ways, and to maintain self and other's face—their positive social values (Goffman, 1967, p. 5)—in doing so (see also Brown & Levinson, 1987). The paradox here is that in the very requirement to *be* something is acknowledgement that one is not simply and already it, that one might be something else, that that which one is "being" is a performance. Of course, a moment from now the situation may shift and the same person may be required to be something else again. At the same time, successful social interaction—ordinarily orderly—requires that people be able to take for granted that they really are who they purport to be. Order requires that people work together to maintain the line of the social interaction. In the early Goffman, this involved primarily facework—efforts to maintain self and other's face—expressions and enactments of deference and demeanor, the sepa-ration of social worlds into frontstage and backstage, with appropriate behaviors constrained to each, rules of politeness, methods for the management of embar-rassment, and so on. These are the ceremonial aspects of everyday encounters. By allocating attention to the needs and disattention to the threats to identity management of self and other, people maintain an uninterrupted smoothness to their interactions, and with it, a reality for their singular self.

Because of the vocabulary of actor, line, face, role, and so on, Goffman has often been interpreted as implying that social life is just a game, social selves just a drama, social reality just a fiction. But this is inadequate to either his work or the realities of social life he was describing. It is not just a game, it is a ritual game, not just a drama but a sacred drama, not just a fiction but a symbolic

constituting of lived-in realities. Careful reading of the early Goffman makes
clear that he is building on Durkheim's provocative, but never fully developed,
ideas about a cult of the individual as a modern secular religion (Chriss, 1993;
Collins, 1988b). The self is the sacred object of the system of interpersonal
interaction; the forms of politeness, deference and demeanor, facework, the
separation of front and backstage behavior, and other such are the rites of approach and avoidance of that sacred object.

Two important points are easily overlooked. One is the moral basis of all of
this. We are dealing here in the world of oughts and ought-nots, specifically,
evaluations of the nature and conduct of the self. Just as for Durkheim, though
by different means, Goffman's social world is constructed of moral imperatives.

Second, this model has as much to do with definition of the situation as
definition of the self. In order that all parties can have a successful social encounter, they must not be liars. That depends on being able to change roles and
identities from moment to moment and situation to situation, without compari-
sons across situations being held up as evaluative criteria. Participants, then,
must cooperate in constructing encounters as relatively sealed off social worlds.
The layer of ceremonial in ordinary interaction, then, is a system of symbolic
forms for ritually constructing morally regulated realities.

Elias's (1939/1978, 1939/1982, 1969/1983) work on the forms of politeness
and civility brings historical and institutional issues to bear. He shows how the
forms of proper interpersonal interaction and public presentation of self have
changed over the history of Europe, and how these historical changes of form
are connected to the institutional structures of the societies in which they appear.
Individual social competence is, then, a form of institutional shaping of individuality. Interestingly, the major trend over the centuries leading up to Western
modernity is the internalization of control, the replacing of institutional force
with individual self-control. (For other historical studies of etiquette, see Bremmer
& Roodenburg, 1991; Kasson, 1990; Koziol, 1992.)

In sum, the identity a person presents is a ritual performance of a position in a
network of social relations and a ritually coordinated sequence of social actions.

11.2

Rituals of Style and Status

Style is that uniqueness that marks texts or performances as characteristic
of a particular group, or authored in a particular time and place by a particular

person. All communicators must make compositional choices; there is seldom a necessary way to say or do something. The choices that are made constitute style. (It is important to recognize that style conceived in this way arises from the redundancy and optionality within sign systems and not from the redundancy within texts. It does not depend on distinguishing the necessary from the unnecessary signs in a given text or performance, and labelling the necessary signs "message" or "information" and the unnecessary signs "style" or "ornamentation"—see sec. 3.4; Shannon & Weaver, 1949/1963. In fact, when conceived as deriving from the redundancy and optionality within sign systems, as distinct from that within texts or performances, style is a *necessity* of texts and performances, for they could not be put together without it.)

If the elements of style correspond to social conventions of performance, they can be seen as ritualization. Certainly when stylistic conventions are used performatively to express some relation, idea, or evaluation of social order (see Handelman, 1990), then we have a clear instance of ritualization.

A particular mode of analysis of subcultural style as ritualistic expression developed in British cultural studies in the 1970s, and has had a wide influence in communication studies (Hall & Jefferson, 1976; Hebdidge, 1979; Willis, 1978). The spectacular subcultures of young males that draw the attention and fear of parents, teachers, the police, and the press—such as bikers, punks, and street gangs—are identified by their clothing, argots, modes of transportation, places of assembly, music, activities, and behavioral styles. These styles and activities are interpreted as modes of expression of social position and attitude vis-à-vis that position, the larger social hierarchy, and the dominant culture. The style, then, is taken to function as a nonlinguistic expressive element of a culture and, at least for the subcultures that these researchers chose for study, the style is seen to be a statement of oppositional politics.

Public visibility is clearly important to the social function of these styles, but visibility alone is not enough.

> Things simply appropriated and worn (or listened to) do not make a style [in the sense intended here]. What makes a style is the activity of stylisation—the active organisation of objects with activities and outlooks, which produce an organised group-identity in the form and shape of a coherent and distinctive way of 'being-in-the-world.' (Clarke, Hall, Jefferson, & Roberts, 1976, p. 54).

There must be homologies (Clarke, 1976, p. 179; Clarke, Hall, Jefferson, & Roberts, 1976, p. 56; Willis, 1978) between the objects of style and the attitudes and group identities, and some effort must be expended on these homologies, on organizing the elements into a system. This is reminiscent of what Weber called elective affinities (e.g., Gerth & Mills, 1946/1958)—logical affinities between cultural and social elements, that become meaningful when they are selected and acted upon.

A brief analysis of elements of the style of American bikers will provide an example. There are a number of homologies among bikers' boots, activities, and ideas. Bikers' boots have a distinct appearance and are functional in riding, when a heavy boot with rubber tread sole planted firmly on the ground is a regularly useful thing. The heaviness of the boots and the way they lower the actual and visual center of gravity of the wearer's body is aesthetically homologous with the heaviness and low center of gravity of Harley-Davidson motorcycles. The heavy boot planted on the ground at the intersection, supporting the resting bike, is opposed by the resting foot propped up on the bike's highway pegs in motion. These light/heavy, still/motion, supporting/supported dichotomies are homologous with other structures of biker thought in which both elements of a contrasting pair are valued, such as community and place versus the road and transientness, loyalty and group membership versus individuality and freedom, and dependability versus spontaneity. These homologies are then acted on in biker culture, creating elective affinities.

The top-versus-bottom and center-of-gravity themes, for example: In the summer bikers normally ride wearing a sleeveless t-shirt. At rallies and other special occasions, a fair number will ride wearing only an open vest and some will ride wearing nothing above the waist. Helmets are universally disdained, their heaviness being the primary complaint; cloth caps and scarves worn pirate style are OK. Bikers never ride without jeans and boots—those who do are not bikers. This is a publicly recognizable style, with an overall impression of more clothes, darker colors, and greater weight below the waist. The complex of utility, aesthetics, semiotic opposition, and metaphor is built into a recognizable style that defines group membership and performs self identity. Its repetitiveness, collective definition, symbolic form, and participation in the serious life mark it as ritualistic.

Similar analyses can be applied to the whole of the worlds of fashion and lifestyle. An important question, though, would be how far the ritual idea can be extended. Hall and Jefferson (1976) and their colleagues used the idea of style as ritual resistance to explore the specific issue of youth cultures whose modes of dressing and acting in public constituted nonverbal and nontraditional political expressions. Though the degree and type of political emphasis will vary and often be irrelevant, analyses that similarly emphasize ritualism could be apt for the study of bikers and other special groups. Fan groups (e.g., for music, sports, soap operas, or science fiction) engage in stylistic behavior readily analyzable by ritual models, as already briefly discussed (sec. 8.2). But given the mundaneness of most people's use of style in everyday life, on the one hand, and the for-profit industries driving the system of fashion, on the other, most scholars have found the ritual idea of some, but limited, utility in studies of fashion and style (e.g., Chaney, 1996; Davis, 1992). In contemporary, industrial societies, ritualistic styles appear to be special cases. One could argue, though, on a continuation of Goffman's work, for a model of cultural competence—albeit within an economy and market—in which lifestyle choices become means for the construction, performance, and display of self, all available to social judgment and, hence, forms of symbolic participation in the serious life.

11.3
Rituals of Contemporary Organizational Life

Organizations are also ripe for ritual analysis. It has often been documented that much of the information gathered by organizations is never used. Research is conducted, reports are written, alternative proposals are examined, much is discussed, but there is evidence that little of it is used to actually inform decision making. At least the information is not used in ways prescribed by information processing principles. The use of the information would not appear to be rational, not adapted to the conditions of the decision-making situation. So all of that information, all of the researching, discussing, and report writing, must have some other symbolic purposes. It has been suggested that they are ritual exercises (Pfeffer, 1981). Similarly, organizational structures, charts of responsibility and information flow, and formal definitions of procedure usually cannot be shown to be either rationally or empirically adequate. Rather, they often appear to be more symbolic and ceremonial (Meyer & Rowan, 1977). As a third example, ritual elements constitute a thick layer in the everyday representation and performance of status, authority, etiquette, and procedure within organizations, as individuals are assigned office space and furniture, as dress codes are performed, greetings given, access controlled, meetings conducted, and reports circulated (Pacanowsky & O'Donnell-Trujillo, 1983).

Recognizing that information processing and much of the formal structure and procedure of organizations are ritual rather than rational processes, it is easy to ridicule. Business leaders are supposed to be rational, but they have people working on things that are never used, their information-gathering labors are empty gestures, the organizational chart is not a chart of something important but of nothing, interactions are more ceremonial than substantive, the whole is mostly symbolic and little real. But such a cynical position is too easy and not informative enough—and, of course, depends on a dichotomizing logic we have already criticized. Better answers come from analyses that are properly attuned to the processes and functions of ritual. For example, Stull, Maynard-Moody, and Mitchell (1988) show that, though the reorganization of bureaucracies has been shown to have little instrumental effect on organizational effectiveness, it is popular and recurrent because it ritualistically opens up opportunities for informal as well as formal change and provides ritual means for producing and legitimizing conflict and change.

Regardless of the instrumental ideology of formal organizations, they are social orders, and thus, rite, ceremony, and the ritual aspects of interaction will serve the same functions in organizations that they do elsewhere in social life. They are a performance of participation. They construct and maintain consensus on at least a few issues. They create and maintain usefully functioning order even in the absence of consensus. They prepare the social group for action. They increase the sense of security (cf. Wallace, 1966).

Ritualistic information gathering and obeisance to formal procedure prepare a group for taking a decision and embarking on the required action. A social group cannot embark on a successful project without a shared sense that the project is well chosen, feasible, worth doing, and so on. As Weber (1922/1978) discusses, this shared confidence could derive from charisma, the gifts of the leader, but much more often it derives from instituted legitimacy. Many, if not most, of the ritual features of organizational life involve the performance of instituted legitimacy.

Pacanowsky and O'Donnell-Trujillo (1983) catalogued many forms of ritual, ceremony, and rite as key parts of organizational communication in the everyday secular life of business organizations, and similar discussions appear in the business and organizational studies literature. Though the family of terms including ritual, rite, ceremony, myth, and symbol appear periodically in analyses of organizational communication, there has been little or no formal follow-up to Pacanowsky and O'Donnel-Trujillo's essay (see Eisenberg, 1990; Kirkwood, 1992 as independent examples). The paradox of regular use of the terms of ritual analysis combined with little formal analytic work devoted to ritual is both based on, and tends to produce, what Knuf (1993) points out is a casual use of "ritual" as a trope rather than as an analytic term. Thus the idea of ritual has failed to produce an intellectual shift in organizational communication studies commensurate with its promise, even when illuminating in particular case studies.

In the larger organizational studies literature, along with even more examples of casual use of the family of ritual terms, there are also some examples of the intellectual payoff produced by more formal and analytical use of the ritual concept. The articles anthologized by Powell and DiMaggio (1991) illustrate how the picture shifts, subtly but decisively, once one begins thinking about organizational life in anthropological ways. Attention to the ritual elements of organizational life alters more general understandings of the organization for both scholars and practitioners. Here are three implications.

Decisions, actions, procedures, and structures can no longer be expected to be purely rational, and the lack of rationality cannot automatically be taken as a fault (e.g., Meyer & Rowan, 1977). If ritual elements are as necessary to life in organizations as they are elsewhere, then part of the organization's resources, part of the time and energy of its people, must inevitably be devoted to actions that follow the logic of ritual and symbol rather than to instrumental calculation. To the extent this is not only an inevitable but a necessary feature of social life, the ritual elements of organizational life should not be eliminated—indeed, they should be understood and, as appropriate, promoted.

Just as the organization cannot be seen as purely instrumentally goal oriented, it cannot be expected to be autonomously responsive to internal mechanisms. Rather, the organization is subject to cultural forces, to the same norms, symbolic logics, and structures of meaning that regulate the ritual elements of life in other domains (e.g., DiMaggio & Powell, 1983; Fairchild, 1989; Friedland & Alford, 1991; Zucker, 1977). Scholars and practitioners, then, must not assume that managers are in charge of all aspects of their organizations, nor that economic forces, or technical or legal changes, are the only elements of the environment of organizations that affect how they work. Organizations are products of their time and place. The ritual elements of life within them are one of the major channels of external influence and control.

Life in the organization must be seen, in part, as a meaningful activity. Organizations and their members have meaningful purposes as well as instrumental goals. Organizations can only be understood by scholars, and successfully run by personnel, who are sensitive to that dimension (Goodsell, 1989; Pacanowski & O'Donnell-Trujillo, 1983). Organizational strategists periodically propose that the fact that people are motivated by symbol and ritual can be used by managers, instrumentally if not cynically, to control workers in ways that will increase the efficiency of the organization (e.g., Bettinger, 1989; Deal & Kennedy, 1982). Such instrumentality not only underestimates the intelligence of the people supposedly so manipulated, but it displays a fundamental misunderstanding of our first two points (cf. Knuf, 1989-90). To turn an instrumental logic on the ritual elements of organizational life is to fail to grasp that the presence of that ritual element is evidence that organizations cannot, any more than any other aspect of life, be adequately understood or run by purely instrumental calculation. Besides, the most important sources of the ritual elements of organizational life are not under the control of organizational managers but are cultural phenomena characteristic of the organization's environment.

12

Ritual Conceptions of
Culture and Communication

B efore concluding discussion of ritual and communication, we must address
some of the larger, most general issues.

First is what might be called the ritualism of world views. Explicitly, here,
we will examine the degree to which modern rationalism and secularism is expressed in ritualistic communication forms. A possible implication is that ritual
is not only ubiquitous—a point that should be clear by now—and it is not only
inevitable, it is necessary. If even anti-ritualism is expressed in ritualistic ways,
perhaps ritualism is a fundamental of human existence.

Second, we turn from these largest matters to their analog among our professional concerns; from world-views we turn to definitions of communication.
The discussion is of the implications of Carey's ritual model of communication.
If all communication is thought of as ritual, what follows for our conduct as
communication scholars?

12.1

The Reformation and the Culture of
Anti-Ritualism as a Matter of Communication Style

Few sociological ideas are as widely accepted as secularization. Though
there are a variety of definitions and uses for the term—a few centuries ago, it
was actually a religious term—in general, secularization is taken to be the historical process by which religious institutions, activities, and thinking lose

predominance in a social order, their influence replaced by competing, secular forms such as science, politics, economics, and administration (see B. R. Wilson, 1987). Evidence of secularization includes (a) decreasing proportions of material wealth, time, and labor devoted to religious institutions and activities, (b) decreasing influence of religious institutions and authorities in politics, economy, public affairs, and everyday life, (c) decreasing deference to religious institutions and authorities by other institutions and authorities, (d) increasing degrees of influence of nonreligious social trends and events on religious activities, and (e) the replacement of religious, supernatural, or magical thinking with empirical and cause-effect thinking, and realist and pragmatic attitudes. Most directly relevant to our concern with ritual, the thesis of secularization implies a historically decreasing prevalence and importance of ritual. Many such trends appear to be characteristic of Western societies during the last 300 or so years, though the particulars are debated (e.g., Barker, Beckford, & Dobbelaere, 1993; B. R. Wilson, 1987). Here we want to introduce two key questions from that literature, and identify evidence of the continuing importance of ritualism, whatever the historical trends of secularization may be.

The first question is whether secularization can be imagined as a process capable of completion, defining historical eras, or whether it is better construed as an internal social dynamic of competition among institutions within historical periods. The former view is a part of the classical sociological idea of modernization, by which religious and other traditional institutions are replaced with capitalist economies and modern, rational politics. But contrary evidence abounds: In the United States, for example, religious institutions are vital—membership and income have actually grown in recent years; around the world, new religious movements appear regularly; religious practices and beliefs continue to be important in family life, and religious institutions provide major rites of passage and holidays (e.g., Bedell, 1996; Caplow, Bahr, & Chadwick, 1983; Stark & Bainbridge, 1985; van Bremen & Martinez, 1995; B. R. Wilson, 1990). This has led to a view of secularization as an ideology as much as a historical description. Scholars' attention is then drawn to the continuing role of religious institutions, activities, and ideas in interaction with others in modern societies (e.g., van Bremen, 1995; Wuthnow, 1988).

The second question is whether the religious aspects of modern life are best addressed by accepting traditional, institutional definitions of religion. A number of scholars have followed Durkheim's (1912/1965) example by adopting a functional definition of religion (cf. B. R. Wilson, 1987; Wuthnow, 1988). This changes questions of secularization fundamentally because then religion is not defined substantively as a specific set—or certain type—of beliefs, practices, or institutions but analytically by reference to certain social functions. "The religious," then, becomes a much larger category than the formal practice of religion, including nationalism, patriotism, or any other set of activities that function for their adherents like religion does for its adherents—for example, in defining cosmologies, values, group membership, and individual identity (e.g., Wallace, 1966). This should be a familiar model as it underlies this book. In this use, the religious is not unlike our category of the serious life. The point here is that functional definitions of religion lead to the conclusion that much of modern life is structured by reference to the religious, even aside from any issues of the role of formal religious institutions (e.g., Cheal, 1992; Thompson, 1990). Hence, as a predominant mode of the religious, ritualism too continues to play key roles in modern life in industrial societies. The ubiquity of ritual is clear from the review of the functions of ritual in the media and in political and other secular settings, thoughout the second half of this book. The performance of ritual in secular life has been implicated in health, happiness, and pathology (e.g., Carlton-Ford, 1992; Cheal, 1992; E. B. Reeves & Bylund, 1989; Wolin, Bennett, Noonan, & Teitelbaum, 1980). Hoover and Venturelli (1996) argue that the media, as predominant expressive social institutions, are one of the major sites for such functionally religious practices, just as we have discussed the media's participation in the serious life, playing essential roles in a variety of ritual activities (see Chs. 9 & 10). We can explore the implications of these issues more deeply by examining the underlying ritualist, and religious, structures of rationalism.

A rationalist approach to ritual presents a paradox. Rationalism presumes that the modern West is in a secular age, that religion, ritual, and magic are no longer of relevance to important things. But indeed, rationalism has its own religious foundations and ritualistic elements. There is evidence in both its origins in the Protestant Reformation and in more recent antiritual attitudes.

In the Protestant Reformation and the intellectual life of premodern and early modern Europe, the idea of the omnipresence of the Christian God's will combined with the idea that His will was a power beyond human intercession formed characteristic attitudes toward the trials and tribulations of everyday life. Events were understood as preordained; human duty was to understand and to cope. This could produce what contemporary readers would see as simple resignation:

> Of course a doctor should try to cure the patient by natural means. But such remedies were to be employed cautiously, with the recognition that they could only work if God permitted. It was lawful to take physic, but unlawful to trust in it too much. . . . Health came from God, not from doctors. (Thomas, 1971, p. 85)

These same ideas laid the groundwork for a natural theology. The world came to be seen as a place where God's will unfolded regularly, rather than being a capricious place where good and evil fought to unpredictable ends. If the world was patterned by divine will, studying the world could be seen as an effort to know God, analogous to studying the Bible. So, as the theology of the Protestant Reformation made the philosophy of Locke and empiricism possible, it prepared the ground for natural science and the naturalistic attitude of modern life.

> The wizards and astrologers lost their prestige during the seventeenth century, whereas the Church has continued into modern times to provide a framework for many of society's activities. But this process was not simply a matter of religion driving out its rivals, for the religion which survived the decline of magic was not the religion of Tudor England. When the Devil was banished to Hell, God himself was confined to working through natural causes. At the end of our period we can draw a distinction between religion and magic which would not have been possible at the beginning. (Thomas, 1971, p. 640)

> Today we think of religion as a belief, rather than a practice, as definable in terms of creeds rather than in modes of behaviour. But such a description would have fitted the popular Catholicism of the Middle Ages little better than it fits many other primitive religions. A medieval peasant's knowledge of Biblical history or Church doctrine was, so far as one can tell, usually extremely slight. The Church was important to him not because of its formalized code of belief, but because its rites were an essential accompaniment to the important events of his own life—birth, marriage and death. It solemnized these occasions by providing appropriate rites of passage to emphasize their social signficance. Religion was a ritual method of living, not a set of dogmas. (Thomas, 1971, p. 76)

One version of history identifies Protestantism and modern science as part of the same self-improving progress. According to this logic, primitive mentality sees the world as a supernatural place and religion as a set of practices. The progress of Western civilization leads to a coming into consciousness by which religion becomes characterized more by belief than by practices and the world is seen as a natural place, regulated by natural laws, available to human investigation. But the modern world we inhabit is not so natural, nor so secular; magic and ritual are not so successfully banished to our primitive past.

First, the Protestant attack on ritual, symbol, and icon was out of proportion, indicating symptomatically that it was ritualistic itself. If their rationalism were simply rational, then witchcraft and the rest would have meant nothing, they would have been nothing to fear. The Puritans, Quakers, and the rest should have just gone their own way; instead they created armies and sailed for new worlds. Indeed, Thomas's (1971) book and other sources are filled with evidence of ritualistic attacks on rituals. The proper ritual attitude was an avoidance of ritual and icon—this is clear in Protestant churches to this day. The Protestants were not creating a world without ritual but a world without what Durkheim (1912/1965) called positive rites. The Protestant world is a world of taboo, a world of ritual avoidance. The point for us is that in such a world, ritual is of no less importance; it is of a different character.

Second, there is a stunning correspondence between Protestantism and positivism. One sees the same iconoclastic venom, the same holy passion, the same emphasis on taboo. Note that positivism is not intended as a label for the practices of empirical researchers in the social sciences today, almost none of whom are genuinely positivist, but as the name of a particular philosophy of science.

> The "Vienna Circle for the Dissemination of the Scientific World-Outlook (*Weltauffassung*)" seeks to create a climate that will be free from metaphysics in order to promote scientific studies in all fields by means of logical analysis. It would be less misleading to speak of a "Vienna Circle for Physicalism," since "world" is a term which does not occur in the language of science, . . . "philosophy" does not exist as a discipline . . . the body of scientific propositions exhausts the sum of all meaningful statements. (Neurath, 1931-32/1959, p. 282)

This is not the dispassionate language by which science moves steadily forward, this is the revolutionary language with which cults are started and cultural wars declared.

There are substantive similarities, too: both positivism and Protestantism are essentially a desire for a plain world. The communicative principles and opportunities for knowledge and authority governing the Quaker meetinghouse and the scientific laboratory and journal have much in common (Peters, 1990). The Vienna Circle desired a whole world ruled by these ideas, as did the first generation of Protestant reformers. The positivists' system of thought—including the declaration that tautologies and verifiable facts constitute the universe of meaningful statements, their resulting claims that metaphysics is a form of lying, and that art and religion are emotive but not meaningful, and their desire for a system of morals that could be reduced to physicalist principles and thereby verifiable facts (see Ayer, 1959, for examples)—is to intellectual life what the Protestant Reformation was to religious life: an attempt to eliminate all but the essentials (as defined by the reformers) and rebuild the whole on the meanest elements of the foundation. The religious zeal can still be seen in the activities of skeptic societies.

Third, we do not actually live in a demystified world, anyway.

> It did not matter that the majority of the population of eighteenth-century England had possibly never heard of Boyle or Newton and certainly could not have explained the nature of their discoveries. At all times most men [and women] accept their basic assumptions on the authority of others. New techniques and attitudes are always more readily diffused than their underlying scientific rationale. . . . Most of those millions of persons who today would laugh at the idea of magic or miracles would have difficulty in explaining why. They are victims of society's constant pressure toward intellectual conformity. Under this pressure the magician has ceased to command respect, and intellectual prestige has shifted elsewhere. (Thomas, 1971, pp. 646-647)

Modern technology gives us control over light and dark, heat and cold, space and time. These technologies may operate by natural means that are scientifically understandable, but we do not experience them that way. Our experience, of listening to the radio for example, shortcircuits the natural working of the technology. Frequency modulation and megahertz are of little importance; the power to alter experiential reality at the flip of a switch is the essential magic. Folding space and time, communication media allow us to bring voices from elsewhere and elsewhen into the present situation (Peters, 1997; Rothenbuhler & Peters, 1997). As Silverstone (1988) puts it regarding television, "there is something peculiarly premodern" about its uses; "our high technology world is essentially a magical one. By whatever mechanism, the boundary between reality and fantasy is constantly being transgressed" (pp. 26-27).

Fourth, though the Protestant Reformation may have forged a religion centered on belief rather than practices and separated the Church from the ritual regulation of everyday life, it did not rid everyday life of the need for ritual regulation. Few may still invoke God's name in greeting and departing—though that is the etymological origin of many common sayings. Most do still say similar things in the same old way, and to the same effect.

Recognizing that ritual is ubiquitous and inevitable, that even anti-ritualism is expressed ritualistically, what we need are scholarly approaches that are sensitive to the enduring value of ritual and prepared to address its communicative forms. We turn now to the analog of world views within the area of our professional concern: General conceptions of communication. Communication conceived as ritual implies a ritualistic world view.

12.2

A Ritual Conception of Communication

new metaphor for comm, ritual vs. transmission [handwritten annotation]

Carey (1975, 1988) is justly famous for proposing a ritual conception of communication, presented as alternative to the purportedly more common transportation or transmission conception. Ritual or transportation are alternative root metaphors, analogies that lie in the backs of our minds as we go about our work as communication scholars. These analogies inform our definitions, vocabularies, models, methods, and explanations, often without our explicit judgment. Carey's claim is that much of the historical and contemporary concern with communication has been dominated by a transportation or transmission metaphor.

The transportation conception of communication emphasizes information and the effectivity of communication across space; the ritual view emphasizes meaning and the maintenance of society in time. One emphasizes power and control, the other participation and culture. This much alone is something important; a pregnant shift in perspectives has been identified. But too often, little more is said and the full value of Carey's idea requires more unpacking than that. Carey's own expositions of these ideas are relatively thin and mostly without example, so I will necessarily be reshaping his ideas to my purposes. What follows, then, is not so much an exposition of Carey's writing as thinking inspired by it.

The first point of this interpretation is a critique of conventional orientations to the study of communication. Transmission, as an implicit root metaphor, causes problems in understanding communication. The second point is a claim about what communication most often does; what the normal human purposes and achievements of entering into communicative relations are. The third point is about the nature of reality, the function of communication in it, and our position in it as scholars.

First, the critique of conventional views: Studies of the effects of communication draw attention away from the meaning of communication. That is a gross generalization, but it focuses attention on an important issue. Instead of the substance of communication, effects studies draw attention to the results—things which, phenomenologically, could be seen to occur outside the communication itself. It is as if concern drifted away from the text to the reader, from the reading to what followed. Following the little arrows in the diagrams of communication effects processes, we move from communication to attitudes and behaviors, from the action to its results.

Further, the concern with communicative effects draws attention to instances of effective communication. Effects become a criterion for allocating attention. Hence, texts that are designed for persuasion, that would produce worrisome persuasive effects, or that are attractive to audiences we fear may be subject to persuasion, are what attract the most attention. To a much lesser degree are texts chosen for their aesthetic richness, hermeneutic possibilities, or historical importance. Because of our greater concern for effects than aesthetics, we study Saturday morning cartoons, pornography, portrayals of violence, and advertising, chosen for their potential deleteriousness rather more than drama, music, or literature chosen for its richness or complexity.

Yet further, the concern for effects has a fragmentary, elementalist tendency about it. As illuminated by a concern with effects, it is easier to see communication as an act than as an interaction, a stimulus than a process. When one is concerned with their results, it is easier to think of things in units and increments. At the very least, when one distinguishes communication from result, one has defined two independent units. Soon one is speaking of communications and their results. At that point the phenomenon of communication activities—the very thickness of everyday life itself—has been conceived as an aggregate of isolable things.

From this point—at which aggregates of communications (or more sophisticatedly, increments of attributes of communications) are said to have degrees of results under specified conditions—it is nearly impossible to get back to the point where communication is understood to be about meaning and aesthetics, self, relation, and social order. In other words, we will be experts on communication who do not conceive it in a way that is useful for the study of how ordinary people—including us—usually use it.

A key part of the problem with conceiving communication as a thing is that the associated metaphors are too physical. If communication is distinguished from result, both treated as things that can come in aggregates or increments, and the purpose of studying them is to assess their association, then communication has been construed as one of two independent units that may or may not exhibit some ordered relation in space and time. (See the criteria for identifying a causal relation in any social science methods text; e.g., do they appear together in all circumstances or only some? do changes in one follow changes in the other?). Though we do not really think there is a transfer of energy from the one to the other, still, once we have isolated, for our attention, two things located in space and time and in some relation to each other, something makes us want to use mechanical-causal terminology as if that were the case, as if one had a significant effect on the other, overcame its inertia, transferred its energy to it. As

Bateson (1972/1987, pp. xxiii-xxvi, 432-473) points out, we have misconstrued human affairs at the most fundamental level when we act as if we expected that their pattern derives from matter and energy the way the pattern of the physical world does.

The differences between thinking of communication as a thing that comes in aggregates, as a variable that comes in amounts, or as a phenomenon exhibiting various characteristics that can in their turn be treated as aggregates or amounts are not as important as their similarity in operationalizing the phenomenon of concern as a thing designated by a noun and isolable in time and space. It seems we can hardly think of such a thing without expecting it to obey the laws of physics.

With the ritual conception of communication, Carey is offering an alternative vision, an alternative language, one much less associated with physical metaphors. If communication is thought of as a ritual rather than a transmission, then it is associated with performance rather than movement, participation rather than consumption, meaning or beauty rather than strategy or results, evocation or calling rather than influence or effectiveness. A ritual is not something one is audience to but something one is participant in. Likewise it is not something that can happen to someone but something one chooses to be a part of. It is not something the meaning of which is above or beyond or behind the backs of its participants—some part of it may be, but in the biggest sense its meaning for the participants is what a ritual is about. We would not try to understand the significance of a ritual by measuring its effects, like we do made-for-TV movies. If we think, then, of all of communication as a ritual, we should be less likely to make that mistake at all.

So that is one part of Carey's inspiration: The ritual conception of communication calls our attention back to the meaning of things. It is a way of thinking about what we study that keeps our attention on its symbolic nature, keeps our mind off of physical metaphors, reminds us of the voluntarism of communication, and won't let us forget to pay attention to the meaning.

A second part of Carey's inspiration calls our attention to what is probably the most common aspect of communication: The expression of commonality, order, stasis. Information deals with difference; most everyday communication has little to do with difference. The news is the same every morning and every evening. The greetings of neighbors and coworkers do not change. Conversation with family members follows familiar patterns. People's interpersonal styles are more the same than different from one day to the next. Familiar TV shows portray familiar characters in familiar plots. It is as if the underlying message of most communication was: Things have not changed.

Very little communication conveys information with the intention of influence and change. Even that which does, such as advertising, is usually performed in terms also indicative of commonality, order, and stasis as Lazarsfeld and Merton (1948) recognized long ago, when they pointed out that most effective persuasion works through the existing order of interpersonal relations or builds on existing beliefs. The change advocated by most persuasive communication is miniscule by comparison to the dramatic portrayal of society as we know it, in which that advocacy is embedded (cf. Goffman, 1976).

The third and most powerful idea held in Carey's ritual conception of communication is, unfortunately, usually overlooked: Communication—ordinary, everyday communication—has the magical, reality-constituting, symbolic-effectivity of all properly performed rituals.

Any instance of communication, Carey points out, has within it both a model of, and a model for, some reality. Just as a sermon makes claims about both how the world works and how we ought to work in it, so does every other bit of communication. The relational aspects of our interpersonal talk do not make simple descriptive claims about who we are and how we stand in relation to each other; they create the symbolic grounds on which we are who we are and how we are related. What the media present as news does not simply describe what is news, it creates what is news. The appeals embedded in advertising are also dramatic portrayals of an imagined world—an imaged world that is treated as natural, taken for granted, existing, and is thereby called into existence. The presence of a given reality among the many that make up the stew of contemporary life is increased by symbolic portrayal on the media, just as it is increased by symbolic portrayal in people's actions. All communication stands in a double relation to the realities of its context: Constituting and commenting. This can be obvious, as in the case of moral imperative, or subtle, as in well crafted drama. But it pervades all.

An important point that Carey delivers about the reality-constituting nature of communication is that we scholars of communication are doing it all the time. Our theories of communication, just like any other bit of communication, contain both models of, and models for, reality—in this case, the reality of communication. Theories of the effects of communication constitute it as an effective phenomenon. Theories of its use constitute it as useful. Theories of rhetoric make it rhetorical. And of course, ritual theories make it ritual.

Lists of alternative conceptions sound arbitrary; attaching those conceptions to differences of reality seems to put us awash in a sea of inconsequence: Pick a conception, pick a reality; don't like what you get, pick another one. But of course the realities about which people care are not ephemeral and inconsequential. Neither are symbols. Symbols could not constitute things called reality unless there were a structural stability to them and their use. The relation of signifier and signified may be *logically* arbitrary, but in everyday use it is a structure. A common but incomplete logic goes like this: Symbols construct reality and symbols are arbitrary, therefore, either (a) reality is arbitrary/ephemeral, or (b) the major premise that symbols construct reality must be wrong. In addressing the symbolic construction of reality, that logic has failed to come to terms with the reality of symbolic construction (Peters & Rothenbuhler, 1989).

The importance of the point that symbols participate in the construction of reality is threefold: First, that they have that structuring power; second, that some part of our reality is, just like symbols, at heart arbitrary; and third, that because symbols, unlike structuring phenomena such as calories and proteins, work through cognitions, people can become aware of the arbitrariness of the relations and choose to change them. The importance of symbolic reality, then, is that it is both a structure and an opportunity for freedom. But freedom is no more capricious than any other reality; it must be a collective response.

If, for example, power is conceived, as is so common, as a zero sum game (see Giddens, 1977; Parsons, 1969 for alternatives) and that conception is embodied in talk and social action, it creates a social world in which one person can only have power at some other person's expense. This is a world in which there must be those that have and those that do not, in which hierarchies must be coercive. Most Americans do conceive of power that way; to a large extent, we do live in such a world. Can some of us then just change our minds? Perhaps yes, but not productively. What is needed is a change of mind by a significant number of people, embodied in a structured set of actions, symbolized in specific and understandable ways, preferably sponsored by an institution of some considerable power. When it comes to discourse about communication by professors of communication this, Carey wants us to remember, is exactly what we've got.

Our talk about communication is socially empowered in a way that others' is not. If we teach students about the conditions of the effectiveness of communication, they will go into the world as practitioners of communication seeking precisely that, effectiveness. Their goal, their criterion of success, will be impact. As Williams (1980, p. 190) asked "What sort of person really wants to 'make an impact' . . . and what state is a society in when this can be its normal cultural language?" How much better, Carey implores, to create with our teaching and research a world in which communication is treasured as a wondrous and magically powerful phenomenon, to be used only very carefully, for only the best of purposes. This is the moral dimension of communication and of ritual; the study of effects alone is too oblivious to it.

To look at the same questions again, from another point of view: When the idea of the social construction of reality is doubled back onto science itself, it is common to think that the power and importance of science have been weakened, because then we are all involved in creating the reality we are attempting to describe. Actually, the power of science has been increased and the importance has become deadly serious. If science—scholarship, more generally—is conducted from some independent point outside of reality and its purpose is to describe it, then if we get it wrong we have just made a mistake and reality will correct us in time. But if scholarship is conducted inside reality and is intimately involved in the whole warp and woof of it all, constituting the conditions of its own descriptions, then if we get it wrong we haven't just made a mistake, we have *created* one—and we must live in it.

13

The Necessity of Ritual to Humane Living

There are three issues to reflect on in conclusion. One is the necessity of ritual to humane living. A second is the necessity of communication theory to understanding how ritual works. A third is the necessity of ritual concepts to the full development of communication scholarship. Much of the book has been devoted to the second and third points; any more reflection is best left to readers. But that first point, though by some lights outside our proper professional scope of concern, is too important to be left without comment. By way of a brief conclusion, let me just state as simply, clearly, and plainly as I can my position on the necessity of ritual to humane living.

How does a ritual work? The individual willfully submits to an external order of signs. We accept the command of the ritual as if it were a material power against which we had none. In fact, it is not. It is an order of signs that has no power without our acceptance. This is what Shils (1980, p. 52) was getting at when he described authority as mind-disturbing. Participation in ritual is the willful subjugation of will; it is the thoughtful acceptance of an imposed order of thought.

This is powerful language; we do not talk about willful subjugation just every day. It is language we are in the habit of thinking only appropriate for the experience of the faithful in religious ritual. As Durkheim (1912/1965) first proposed and many others reviewed in this volume have demonstrated, however, other social situations function in the way religious ritual does for the faithful. National rituals for the patriotic, relationship rituals for the romantic, friendship rituals for the loyal, authority rituals for the obedient, rituals of politeness for

129

the civil, all are examples of the willful subjection of the self to an external order of signs with community sanction. Rituals show up in small ways, they are sprinkled throughout our everyday interactions. We are in the habit of such things and seldom think about them, but there they are.

Does this unthoughtfulness, this surrender of autonomy mean that ritual is bad? Certainly it appears out of keeping with the tradition of rationalism. Were we to think about it, as we do in religious situations, it would require Kierkegaard's leap of faith. Ritual requires that we set aside our own cognitive facilities and accept the programmed order. Should I nod hello? Ask how you are? Do you mean me any harm? Should I adopt a position of threat? No, in order to perform civil society, we must leap across the chasm of our doubts, banish such questions from our minds, and lose ourselves in the performance. We must not just act civil (though that will do in a pinch and is good enough for teaching children) on an everyday basis, if we are to live up to our obligations, we must *be* civil. It is mind numbing, but we only experience the numbness when we reflect on our lost choices. How often do we find the rules of politeness, or the sway of authority, more powerful than our desire to frankly express our passions, to challenge our colleagues, to upset the working order? This quality makes ritual a powerful tool for authority; the same quality makes ritual necessary for sociality.

Ritual is necessary to social order. It is the symbolic means of crafting the self in social shape, of putting the will in the order of the social. Without it we would have no means of social order between happy cooperation, rational agreement, and brute coercion. Real life, so far as we know, cannot always be happy and cooperative—the world we live in is too big for rational agreements among all the interested parties. But neither do we want our world to be brutally coercive. Some may call ritual a type of symbolic coercion, just brutality in another form. But I prefer it: that difference in form is a difference that makes a difference. The symbolic form of ritual requires the individual's acceptance, it always allows for reinterpretation, it is reasonably open to change, and resistance does not require bloodshed. For sure, some rituals will be as bad as the worst of the social order in which they work. Others in the same inequitable society will be about ideals that model a better social order and call for improvement in the existing one. We have no evidence that we can live apart and plenty that we can only live together. Ritual is a means for managing that.

Finally, ritual is a means for individual participation in greater things, larger orders, more fundamental realities. The religious impulse is a constant of human history, only its substances are as various as the contexts of its expression. Humans everywhere place themselves symbolically in orders of important things; we use rituals for that. In different contexts, from religion to nationalism, social relations to organizational obligations, rituals put us in contact with ideas— values, truths, narratives, meanings—that are larger than we, that enrich our lives by their largeness. These ideas have, in ritual, a self-evident seriousness, for they appear through the window of the ritual as existing before and after the contact, indeed, as outside our ordinary realm. This is language we inherited from religion, but this numinous contact with the sacred is a better part of the life of everyone who strives to be honest, who values the truth, who responds to a calling for greater loyalty, greater creativity, greater intelligence, or greater good.

Ritual is powerful and, like all powers, it is dangerous. It is also enriching and humane, a means for the communicative construction of social order, for the meaningful management of social relations.

References

Abrahams, R. D. (1983). *The man of words in the West Indies: Performance and the emergence of Creole culture.* Baltimore: Johns Hopkins Press.

Alexander, B. (1987). Ceremony. *Encyclopedia of religion* (Vol.3, pp. 179-183). New York: Macmillan.

Alexander, B. (1991). *Victor Turner revisited: Ritual as social change.* Atlanta, GA: Scholars Press.

Alexander, J. C. (1978). Formal and substantive voluntarism in the work of Talcott Parsons: A theoretical and ideological reinterpretation. *American Sociological Review, 43,* 177-198.

Alexander, J. C. (1982). *Theoretical logic in sociology: Vol.1. Positivism, presuppositions, and current controversies.* Berkeley: University of California Press.

Alexander, J. C. (1984). Three models of culture and society relations: Toward an analysis of Watergate. *Sociological Theory, 3,* 290-314.

Alexander, J. C. (1988a). Culture and political crisis: "Watergate" and Durkheimian sociology. In J. C. Alexander (Ed.), *Durkheimian sociology: Cultural studies* (pp. 187-224). Cambridge: Cambridge University Press.

Alexander, J. C. (Ed.). (1988b). *Durkheimian sociology: Cultural studies.* Cambridge: Cambridge University Press.

Altman, R. (1987). Television sound. In H. Newcomb (Ed.), *Television: The critical view* (4th ed.) (pp. 566-584). New York: Oxford University Press.

Anderson, J. A., & Meyer, T. P. (1988). *Mediated communication: A social action perspective.* Newbury Park, CA: Sage.

Austin, J. L. (1975). *How to do things with words.* Cambridge, MA: Harvard University Press. (Original work published 1962)

Ayer, A. J. (Ed.). (1959). *Logical positivism.* New York: Free Press.

Bak, J. M. (Ed.). (1990). *Coronations: Medieval and early modern monarchic ritual.* Berkeley: University of California Press.

Baker, J. H. (1983). *Affairs of party: The political culture of Northern Democrats in the mid-nineteenth century.* Ithaca, NY: Cornell University Press.

Baran, S. J., & Blasko, V. J. (1984). Social perceptions and the by-products of advertising. *Journal of Communication, 34*(3), 12-20.

Barker, B. (1979). *The symbols of sovereignty.* Oxford: Westbridge Books.

Barker, E., Beckford, J. A., & Dobbelaere, K. (Eds.). (1993). *Secularization, rationalism, and sectarianism: Essays in honor of Bryan R. Wilson.* Oxford: Clarendon Press.

Barthes, R. (1968). *Elements of semiology* (A. Lavers & C. Smith, Trans.). New York: Hill & Wang. (Original work published 1964)

Barthes, R. (1972). *Mythologies* (A. Lavers, Trans.). New York: Hill and Wang. (Original work published 1957)

Bateson, G. (1987). *Steps to an ecology of mind: Collected essays in anthropology, psychiatry, evolution, and epistemology.* Northvale, NJ: Jason Aronson. (Original work published 1972)

Bauman, R. (1977). *Verbal art as performance.* Rowley, MA: Newbury House.

Bauman, R. (1989). Performance. In E. Barnouw (Ed.), *International Encyclopedia of Communications* (Vol. 3, pp. 262-266). New York: Oxford University Press.

Bauman, R., & Briggs, C. L. (1990). Poetics and performance as critical perspectives on language and social life. *Annual Review of Anthropology, 19,* 59-88.

Becker, H. S. (1982). *Art Worlds.* Berkeley: University of California Press.

Becker, K. (1995). Media and the ritual process. *Media, Culture, and Society, 17,* 629-646.

Bedell, K. B. (Ed.). (1996). *Yearbook of American and Canadian churches, 1996.* Nashville, TN: Abingdon Press.

Belk, R. W., Wallendorf, M., & Sherry, J. F. (1989). The sacred and the profane in consumer behavior: Theodicy on the odyssey. *Journal of Consumer Research, 16,* 1-38.

Bell, C. (1992). *Ritual theory, ritual practice.* New York: Oxford University Press.

Bellah, R. N. (1970). Civil religion in America. In R. N. Bellah, *Beyond belief: Essays on religion in a post-traditional world* (pp. 168-189). New York: Harper & Row.

Bennett, W. L. (1977). The ritualistic and pragmatic bases of political campaign discourse. *Quarterly Journal of Speech, 63,* 219-238.

Bettinger, C. (1989). Use corporate culture to trigger high performance. *Journal of Business Strategy, 10 (March-April),* 38-42.

Bird, S. E., & Dardenne, R. W. (1988). Myth, chronicle, and story: Exploring the narrative qualities of news. In J. W. Carey (Ed.), *Media, myths, and narratives: Television and the press* (pp. 67-86). Newbury Park, CA: Sage.

Birrell, S. (1981). Sport as ritual: Interpretations from Durkheim to Goffman. *Social Forces, 60,* 354-376.

Bloch, M. (Ed.). (1975). *Political language and oratory in traditional society.* New York: Academic Press.

Bloch, M. (1989). *Ritual, history, and power: Selected papers in anthropology* (London School of Economics Monographs on Social Anthropology No. 58). London: Athlone Press.

Boorstin, D. (1961). *The image: A guide to pseudo-events in America.* New York: Atheneum.

Bossard, J. H. S., & Boll, E. S. (1950). *Ritual in family living: A contemporary study.* Philadelphia, PA: University of Pennsylvania Press.

Bremmer, J., & Roodenburg, H. (Eds.). (1991). *A cultural history of gesture.* Ithaca, NY: Cornell University Press.

Brown, P., & Levinson, S. C. (1987). *Politeness: Some universals in language usage.* Cambridge: Cambridge University Press.

Browne, R. B., (Ed.). (1980). *Rituals and ceremonies in popular culture.* Bowling Green, OH: Bowling Green University Press.

Brownell, S. E. (1993). Qing dynasty grand sacrifice and communist national sports games: Rituals of the Chinese state? *Journal of Ritual Studies, 7,* 45-63.

Bryant, D. C. (1953). Rhetoric: Its function and scope. *Quarterly Journal of Speech, 39,* 401-424.

Burgess, T. C. (1987). *Epideictic literature.* New York: Garland. (Original work published 1902)

Burke, K. (1966). *Language as symbolic action: Essays on life, literature, and method.* Berkeley: University of California Press.

Burke, K. (1970). *The rhetoric of religion: Studies in logology.* Berkeley: University of California Press. (Original work published 1961)

Burke, K. (1973). *The philosophy of literary form: Studies in symbolic action* (3rd ed.). Berkeley: University of California Press.

Burke, K. (1989). *On symbols and society* (J. R. Gusfield, Ed.). Chicago: University of Chicago Press.

Buxton, D. (1990). Rock music, the star system, and the rise of consumerism. In S. Frith & A. Goodwin (Eds.), *On record: Rock, pop, and the written word* (pp. 427-440). New York: Pantheon Books.

Camic, C. (1986). The matter of habit. *American Journal of Sociology, 91,* 1039-1087.

Cannadine, D. (1983). The context, performance, and meaning of ritual: The British monarchy and the "invention of tradition," c. 1820-1977. In E. Hobsbawm & R. Ranger (Eds.), *The invention of tradition* (pp. 101-164). New York: Cambridge University Press.

Cannadine, D., & Price, S. (Eds.). (1987). *Rituals of royalty: Power and ceremonial in traditional societies.* Cambridge: Cambridge University Press.

Caplow, T. (1984). Rule enforcement without visible means: Christmas gift giving in Middletown. *American Journal of Sociology, 89,* 1306-1323.

Caplow, T., Bahr, H. M., & Chadwick, B. A. (1983). *All faithful people: Change and continuity in Middletown's religion.* Minneapolis: University of Minnesota Press.

Caplow, T., Bahr, H. M., Chadwick, B. A., Hill, R., & Williamson, M. H. (1983). *Middletown families: Fifty years of change and continuity.* New York: Bantam Books.

Carey, J. (1969). Harold Adams Innis and Marshall McLuhan. In R. Rosenthal (Ed.), *McLuhan: Pro and con* (pp. 270-308). New York: Penguin.

Carey, J. (1975). A cultural approach to communication. *Communication, 2,* 1-22.

Carey, J. (1981). McLuhan and Mumford: The roots of modern media analysis. *Journal of Communication, 31*(3), 162-178.

Carey, J. (1988). *Communication as culture: Essays on media and society.* Boston: Unwin Hyman.

Carlton-Ford, S. L. (1992). Charisma, ritual, collective effervescence, and self-esteem. *Sociological Quarterly, 33,* 565-387.

Carnes, M. C. (1989). *Secret ritual and manhood in Victorian America.* New Haven, CN: Yale University Press.

Carstairs, G. M. (1966). Ritualization of roles in sickness and healing. *Philosophical transactions of the Royal Society of London, 251* (Series B, 772), 305-309.

Carter, M. F. (1991). The ritual functions of epideictic rhetoric: The case of Socrates' funeral oration. *Rhetorica, 9,* 209-232.

Chaffee, L. (1993). Dramaturgical politics: The culture and ritual of demonstrations in Argentina. *Media, Culture, and Society, 15,* 113-135.

Chaney, D. (1983). A symbolic mirror of ourselves: Civic ritual in mass society. *Media, Culture, and Society, 5,* 119-135.

Chaney, D. (1986). The symbolic form of ritual in mass communication. In P. Golding, G. Murdock, & P. Schlesinger (Eds.), *Communicating politics: Mass communications and the political process* (pp. 115-132). New York: Holmes & Meier.

Chaney, D. (1993). *Fictions of collective life: Public drama in late modern culture.* New York: Routledge.

Chaney, D. (1996). *Lifestyles.* New York: Routledge.

Cheal, D. J. (1988). Relationships in time: Ritual, social structure, and the life course. *Studies in Symbolic Interaction, 9,* 83-109.

Cheal, D. J. (1992). Ritual: Communication in action. *Sociological Analysis, 53,* 363-374.

Chriss, J. J. (1993). Durkheim's cult of the individual as a civil religion: Its appropriation by Erving Goffman. *Sociological Spectrum, 13,* 251-275.

Clarke, J. (1976). Style. In S. Hall & T. Jefferson (Eds.), *Resistance through rituals: Youth subcultures in post-war Britain* (pp. 175-191). London: Unwin Hyman.

Clarke, J., Hall, S., Jefferson, T., & Roberts, B. (1976). Subcultures, cultures and class: A theoretical overview. In S. Hall & T. Jefferson (Eds.), *Resistance through rituals: Youth subcultures in post-war Britain* (pp. 9-79). London: Unwin Hyman.

Cmiel, K. (1994). The politics of civility. In D. Farber (Ed.), *The sixties: From memory to history* (pp. 263-290). Chapel Hill: University of North Carolina Press.

Coates, J. (1996). *Women talk: Conversation between women friends.* Oxford: Blackwell.

Collins, R. (1986). The passing of intellectual generations: Reflections on the death of Erving Goffman. *Sociological Theory, 4,* 106-113.

Collins, R. (1988a). The Durkheimian tradition in conflict sociology. In J. C. Alexander (Ed.), *Durkheimian sociology: Cultural studies* (pp. 107-128). New York: Cambridge University Press.

Collins, R. (1988b). Theoretical continuities in Goffman's work. In P. Drew & A. Wootton (Eds.), *Erving Goffman: Exploring the interaction order* (pp. 41-63). Cambridge: Polity Press.

Cooper, D., & Worden, S. (1989). Patriotic symbols in newly-independent nations: A framework for analysis. *Humanity and Society, 13,* 327-343.

Coupland, J., Coupland, N., & Robinson, J. D. (1992). "How are you?": Negotiating phatic communion. *Language in Society, 21,* 207-230.

Crawford, M. (1995). *Talking difference: On gender and language.* Thousand Oaks, CA: Sage.

Cressy, D. (1990). Death and the social order: The funerary preferences of Elizabethan gentlemen. *Continuity and Change, 5,* 99-119.

Davis, F. (1992). *Fashion, culture, and identity.* Chicago: University of Chicago Press.

Dayan, D., & Katz, E. (1988). Articulating consensus: The ritual and rhetoric of media events. In J. C. Alexander (Ed.), *Durkheimian sociology: Cultural studies* (pp. 161-186). Cambridge: Cambridge University Press.

Dayan, D., & Katz, E. (1992). *Media events: The live broadcasting of history.* Cambridge: Harvard University Press.

Dayan, D., Katz, E., & Kerns, P. (1984). Armchair pilgrimages: The trips of Pope John Paul II and their television public. *On Film, 13,* 25-34.

Deal, T., & Kennedy, A. (1982). *Corporate cultures: The rites and rituals of corporate life.* Reading, MA: Addison-Wesley.

Debord, G. (1977). *Society of the spectacle* (rev. ed.). Detroit: Black & Red Press.

deCordova, R. (1990). *Picture personalities: The emergence of the star system in America.* Urbana: University of Illinois Press.

Della Fave, L. R. (1991). Ritual and the legitimation of inequality. *Sociological Perspectives, 34,* 21-38.

Deutscher, I. (1959). *The prophet unarmed: Trotsky, 1921-1929.* New York: Vintage.

Dilthey, W. (1976). *Selected writings* (H. P. Rickman, Ed.). Cambridge: Cambridge University Press.

Dilthey, W. (1989). *Selected works, Volume I: Introduction to the human sciences* (R. A. Makkreel & R. Rodi, Eds.). Princeton, NJ: Princeton University Press.

DiMaggio, P. J., & Powell, W. W. (1983). The iron cage revisited: Institutional isomorphism and collective rationality in organizational fields. *American Sociological Review, 48,* 147-160.

Dinges, W. D. (1987). Ritual conflict as social conflict: Liturgical reform in the Roman Catholic Church. *Sociological Analysis, 48,* 138-157.

Dirks, R. (1988). Annual rituals of conflict. *American Anthropologist, 90,* 856-870.

Doob, A. N., & MacDonald, G. E. (1979). Television viewing and fear of victimization: Is the relationship causal? *Journal of Personality and Social Psychology, 37,* 170-179.

Douglas, M. (1978). *Purity and danger: An analysis of the concepts of pollution and taboo.* London: Routledge & Kegan Paul. (Original work published 1966)

Douglas, M. (1982). *Natural symbols: Explorations in cosmology.* New York: Pantheon. (Original work published 1970)

Douglas, M. (1980). *Edward Evans-Pritchard.* New York: Viking.

Douglass, F. (1996). What to the slave is the Fourth of July? In W. L. Andrews (Ed.), *The Oxford Frederick Douglass Reader* (pp. 108-130). New York: Oxford University Press.

Drew, P., & Wootton, A. (Eds.). (1988). *Erving Goffman: Exploring the interaction order.* Cambridge: Polity Press.

Durkheim, É. (1965). *The elementary forms of the religious life* (J. W. Swain, Trans.). New York: Free Press. (Original work published 1912)

Durkheim, É. (1973). *Moral education* (E. K. Wilson & H. Schnurer, Trans.). New York: Free Press. (Original work published 1925)

Durkheim, É. (1982). *The rules of sociological method* (S. Lukes, Ed., W. D. Halls, Trans.). New York: The Free Press. (Original work published 1895)

Durkheim, É. (1983). *Professional ethics and civic morals* (C. Brookfield, Trans.). Westport, CN: Greenwood Press. (Original work published 1958)

Durkheim, É. (1984). *The division of labor in society* (W. D. Halls, Trans.). New York: Free Press. (Original work published 1893)

Durkheim, É., & Mauss, M. (1963). *Primitive classification* (R. Needham, Ed. & Trans.). Chicago: University of Chicago Press. (Original work published 1903)

Dyer, R. (1979). *Stars.* London: British Film Institute.

Eason, D. L. (1988). On journalistic authority: The Janet Cooke scandal. In J. W. Carey (Ed.), *Media, myths, and narratives: Television and the press* (pp. 205-227). Newbury Park, CA: Sage.

Eastman, S. T., & Riggs, K. E. (1994). Televised sports and ritual: Fan experiences. *Sociology of Sport Journal, 11,* 249-274.

Eibl-Eibesfeldt, I. (1975). *Ethology: The biology of behavior* (2nd ed.). New York: Holt, Rinehart & Winston.

Eisenberg, E. M. (1990). Jamming: Transcendence through organizing. *Communication Research, 17,* 139-164.

Eliade, M. (1959). *The sacred and the profane: The nature of religion.* New York: Harcourt Brace Jovanovich.

Eliade, M. (1991). *Images and symbols: Studies in religious symbolism* (P. Mairet, Trans.). Princeton: Princeton University Press. (Original work published 1952)

Eliade, M., & Sullivan, L. E. (1987). Hierophany. *Encyclopedia of religion,* (Vol. 6, pp. 313-317). New York: Macmillan.

Elias, N. (1978). *The civilizing process, Vol. 1: The history of manners* (E. Jephcott, Trans.). New York: Pantheon Books. (Original work published 1939)

Elias, N. (1982). *The civilizing process, Vol. 2: Power and civility* (E. Jephcott, Trans.). New York: Pantheon Books. (Original work published 1939)

Elias, N. (1983). *The court society* (E. Jephcott, Trans.). New York: Pantheon Books. (Original work published 1969)

Elliott, P. (1982). Media performance as political ritual. *Communication, 7,* 115-130.

Emerson, M. B., & Perse, E. M. (1995). Media events and sports orientations to the 1992 Winter Olympics. *The Journal of International Communication, 2,* 80-99.

Etkin, W. (1967). Theories of animal socialization and communication. In W. Etkin & D. G. Freedman, *Social behavior from fish to man* (pp. 74-111). Chicago: University of Chicago Press.

Ettema, J. S. (1990). Press rites and race relations: A study of mass-mediated ritual. *Critical Studies in Mass Communication, 7,* 309-331.

Evans-Pritchard, E. E. (1962). *Social anthropology and other essays.* Glencoe, IL: Free Press.

Evans-Pritchard, E. E. (1965). *Theories of primitive religion.* Oxford: Clarendon Press.

Evans-Pritchard, E. E. (1981). *A history of anthropological thought.* London: Faber & Faber.

Fairchild, E. (1989). National culture and police organizations in Germany and the United States. *Public Administration Review, 49,* 454-462.

Farrell, T. B. (1978). Political conventions as legitimation ritual. *Communication Monographs, 45,* 293-305.

Farrell, T. B. (1989). Media rhetoric as social drama: The Winter Olympics of 1984. *Critical Studies in Mass Communication, 6,* 158-182.

Finnegan, R. (1969). How to do things with words: Performative utterances among the Limba of Sierra Leone. *Man, 4* (new series), 537-551.

Firth, R. (1963). *Elements of social organization* (3rd ed.). Boston: Beacon.

Firth, R. (1972). Verbal and bodily rituals of greeting and parting. In J. S. La Fontaine (Ed.), *The interpretation of ritual: Essays in honour of A. I. Richards* (pp. 1-38). London: Tavistock Publications.

Firth, R. (1973). *Symbols: Public and private.* Ithaca, NY: Cornell University Press.

Fish, S. (1980). *Is there a text in this class? The authority of interpretive communities.* Cambridge, MA: Harvard University Press.

Foley, D. E. (1990). The great American football ritual: Reproducing race, class, and gender inequality. *Sociology of Sport Journal, 7,* 111-135.

Fortes, M., & Evans-Pritchard, E. E., (Eds.). (1940). *African political systems.* London: Oxford University Press.

Frese, P. R. (1993). *Celebrations of identity: Multiple voices in American ritual performance.* Westport, CN: Bergin & Garvey.

Freud, S. (1937). *The interpretation of dreams* (8th ed., G. S. Hall, Trans.). London: George Allen & Unwin. (Original work published 1913)

Freud, S. (1950). *Totem and taboo* (J. Strachey, Ed. & Trans.). New York: W. W. Norton. (Original work published 1913)

Freud, S. (1959). *Group psychology and the analysis of the ego* (J. Strachey, Ed. & Trans.). New York: W. W. Norton. (Original work published 1921)

Freud, S. (1961). *The future of an illusion* (J. Strachey, Ed. & Trans.). New York: W. W. Norton. (Original work published 1928)

Freud, S. (1961). *Civilization and its discontents* (J. Strachey, Ed. & Trans.). New York: W. W. Norton. (Original work published 1930)

Freud, S. (1964). *Moses and monotheism* (J. Strachey, Ed. & Trans.). New York: W. W. Norton. (Original work published 1939)

Friedland, R., & Alford, R. R. (1991). Bringing society back in: Symbols, practices, and institutional contradictions. In W. W. Powell & P. J. DiMaggio (Eds.), *The new institutionalism in organizational analysis* (pp. 232-263). Chicago: University of Chicago Press.

Gadamer, H. (1975). *Truth and method.* New York: Crossroad Publishing. (Original work published 1960)

Gainer, B. (1995). Ritual and relationships: Interpersonal influences on shared consumption. *Journal of Business Research, 32,* 253-260.

Gay, V. P. (1979). *Freud on ritual: Reconstruction and critique.* Missoula, MT: Scholars Press.

Geertz, C. (1973). *The interpretation of cultures.* New York: Basic Books.

Geertz, C. (1977). Centers, kings, and charisma: Reflections on the symbolics of power. In J. Ben-David & T. N. Clark (Eds.), *Culture and its creators: Essays in honor of Edward Shils* (pp. 150-171). Chicago: University of Chicago Press.

Geertz, C. (1980). *Negara: The theatre state in nineteenth-century Bali.* Princeton, NJ: Princeton University Press.

Gellner, E. (1981). Introduction. In E. Evans-Pritchard (Ed.), *A history of anthropological thought* (pp. xiii-xxxvi). London: Faber.

Gennep, A. van (1960). *The rites of passage* (M. B. Vizedom & G. L. Caffee, Trans.). Chicago: University of Chicago Press. (Original work published 1908)

Gerbner, G. (1984). Science or ritual dance? A revisionist view of television violence research. *Journal of Communication, 34* (3), 164-173.

Gerbner, G., & Gross, L. (1976). Living with television: The violence profile. *Journal of Communication, 26*(2), 173-199.

Gerbner, G., Gross, L., Morgan, M., & Signorielli, N. (1982). Charting the mainstream: Television's contributions to political orientations. *Journal of Communication, 32*(2), 100-127.

Gerbner, G., Gross, L., Morgan, M., & Signorielli, N. (1986). Living with television: The dynamics of the cultivation process. In J. Bryant & D. Zillmann (Eds.), *Perspectives on media effects* (pp. 17-40). Hillsdale, NJ: Lawrence Erlbaum.

Gerth, H. H., & Mills, C. W. (Eds.). (1958). *From Max Weber: Essays in sociology* (H. H. Gerth & C. W. Mills, Trans.). New York: Oxford University Press. (Original work published 1946)

Giddens, A. (1977). "Power" in the writings of Talcott Parsons: Remarks on the theory of power. In A. Giddens (Ed.), *Studies in social and political theory* (pp. 333-349). New York: Basic Books.

Giddens, A. (1988). Goffman as a systematic social theorist. In P. Drew & A. Wootton (Eds.), *Erving Goffman: Exploring the interaction order* (pp. 250-279). Cambridge: Polity Press.

Gilligan, C. (1982). *In a different voice.* Cambridge, MA: Harvard University Press.

Gillis, J. R. (Ed.). (1994). *Commemorations: The politics of national identity.* Princeton, NJ: Princeton University Press.

Gluckman, M. (1955). *Custom and conflict in Africa.* Oxford: Blackwell.

Gluckman, M. (1962). Les rites de passage. In M. Gluckman (Ed.), *Essays on the ritual of social relations* (pp. 1-52). Manchester: Manchester University Press.

Gluckman, M. (1963). *Order and rebellion in tribal Africa.* New York: Free Press.

Goethals, G. T. (1981). *The TV ritual: Worship at the video altar.* Boston: Beacon Press.

Goethals, G. T. (1985). Religious communication and popular piety. *Journal of Communication, 35*(1), 149-156.

Goffman, E. (1959). *The presentation of self in everyday life.* New York: Anchor Books.

Goffman, E. (1963a). *Behavior in public places: Notes on the social organization of gatherings.* New York: Free Press.

Goffman, E. (1963b). *Stigma: Notes on the management of spoiled identity.* Englewood Cliffs, NJ: Prentice-Hall.

Goffman, E. (1967). *Interaction ritual: Essays on face-to-face behavior.* New York: Anchor Books.

Goffman, E. (1971). *Relations in public: Microstudies of the public order.* New York: Harper & Row.

Goffman, E. (1974). *Frame analysis: An essay on the organization of experience.* Cambridge, MA: Harvard University Press.

Goffman, E. (1976). *Gender advertisements.* New York: Harper & Row.

Goffman, E. (1981). *Forms of talk.* Oxford: Blackwell.

Goffman, E. (1983a). Felicity's condition. *American Journal of Sociology, 89,* 1-53.

Goffman, E. (1983b). The interaction order: American Sociological Association, 1982 Presidential Address. *American Sociological Review, 48,* 1-17.

Gold, E. R. (1978). Political apologia: The ritual of self-defense. *Communication Monographs, 45,* 306-316.

Gombrich, E. H. (1966). Ritualized gesture and expression in art. *Philosophical transactions of the royal society of London, 251* (Series B, 772), 393-401.

Goodman, F. D. (1988). *Ecstasy, ritual, and alternate reality: Religion in a pluralistic world.* Bloomington: Indiana University Press.

Goodsell, C. T. (1989). Administration as ritual. *Public Administration Review, 49,* 161-166.

Goody, J. (1961). Religion and ritual: The definitional problem. *British Journal of Sociology, 12,* 142-164.

Goody, E. (1972). Greeting, begging, and the presentation of respect. In J. S. La Fontaine (Ed.), *The interpretation of ritual: Essays in honour of A. I. Richards* (pp. 39-71). London: Tavistock Publications.

Goody, J. (1977). Against "ritual": Loosely structured thoughts on a loosely defined topic. In S. F. Moore & B. G. Myerhoff (Eds.), *Secular ritual* (pp. 25-35). Amsterdam: Van Gorcum.

Gramsci, A. (1971). *Selections from the prison notebooks* (Q. Hoare & G. N. Smith, Eds. & Trans.). New York: International Publishers.

Greenberg, B. S., & Parker, E. B. (1965). *The Kennedy assassination and the American public.* Stanford, CA: Stanford University Press.

Gregory, S. W. (1994). Sounds of power and deference: Acoustic analysis of macro social constraints on micro interaction. *Sociological Perspectives, 37,* 497-526.

Grimes, R. L. (1987). Ritual studies. *Encyclopedia of religion* (Vol. 12, pp. 422-425). New York: Macmillan.

Grimes, R. L. (1990). *Ritual criticism: Case studies in its practice, essays on its theory.* Columbia: University of South Carolina Press.

Grimes, R. L. (1995). *Beginnings in ritual studies* (rev. ed.). Columbia: University of South Carolina Press.

Gronbeck, B. E. (1978a). The functions of Presidential campaigning. *Communication Monographs, 45,* 268-280.

Gronbeck, B. E. (1978b). The rhetoric of political corruption: Sociolinguistic, dialectical, and ceremonial processes. *Quarterly Journal of Speech, 64,* 155-172.

Gronbeck, B. E. (1981). McLuhan as rhetorical theorist. *Journal of Communication, 31*(3), 117-128.

Gronbeck, B. E. (1986). Ronald Reagan's enactment of the presidency in his 1981 inaugural address. In H. W. Simons & A. A. Aghzarian (Eds.), *Form, genre, and the study of political discourse* (pp. 226-245). Columbia: University of South Carolina Press.

Gronbeck, B. E. (1991). The rhetorical studies tradition and Walter J. Ong: Oral-literacy theories of mediation, culture, and consciousness. In B. E. Gronbeck, T. J. Farrell, & P. A. Soukup (Eds.), *Media, consciousness, and culture: Explorations of Walter Ong's thought* (pp. 5-24). Newbury Park, CA: Sage.

Gusfield, J. R., & Michalowicz, J. (1984). Secular symbolism: Studies of ritual, ceremony, and the symbolic order in modern life. *Annual Review of Sociology, 10,* 417-435.

Haines, D. W. (1988). Ritual or ritual? Dinnertime and Christmas among some ordinary American families. *Semiotica, 68,* 75-88.

Halbwachs, M. (1992). *On collective memory* (L. A. Coser, Ed. & Trans.). Chicago: University of Chicago Press.

Hall, S., & Jefferson, T. (Eds.). (1976). *Resistance through rituals: Youth subcultures in post-war Britain.* London: Unwin Hyman.

Hallin, D. C., & Gitlin, T. (1993). Agon and ritual: The Gulf War as popular culture and as television drama. *Political Communication, 10,* 411-424.

Handelman, D. (1990). *Models and mirrors: Towards an anthropology of public events.* Cambridge: Cambridge University Press.

Harris, M. (1968). *The rise of anthropological theory.* New York: Harper & Row.

Harrison, J. E. (1913). *Ancient art and ritual.* New York: Henry Holt.

Hebdidge, D. (1979). *Subculture: The meaning of style.* London: Methuen.

Hinde, R. A. (1982). *Ethology: Its nature and relations with other sciences.* New York: Oxford University Press.

Hirsch, P. M. (1980). The "scary world" of the nonviewer and other anomalies: A reanalysis of Gerbner *et al.*'s findings on cultivation analysis. *Communication Research, 7,* 403-456.

Hoban, J. L., Jr. (1980). Rhetorical rituals of rebirth. *Quarterly Journal of Speech, 66,* 275-288.

Hobsbawm, E., & Ranger, T. (Eds.). (1983). *The invention of tradition.* Cambridge: Cambridge University Press.

Hoover, S. M. (1988). Television myth and ritual: The role of substantive meaning and spatiality. In J. W. Carey (Ed.), *Media, myths, and narratives: Television and the press,* (pp. 161-178). Newbury Park, CA: Sage.

Hoover, S. M., & Venturelli, S. S. (1996). The category of the religious: The blindspot of contemporary media theory? *Critical Studies in Mass Communication, 13,* 251-265.

Hoxie, R. G. (1993). Inaugurating the presidency and the president. *Presidential Studies Quarterly, 23,* 213-219.

Hunt, E. (1977). Ceremonies of confrontation and submission: The symbolic dimension of Indian-Mexican political interaction. In S. F. Moore & B. G. Myerhoff (Eds.), *Secular ritual* (pp. 124-147). Amsterdam: Van Gorcum.

Hunt, L. (1988). The sacred and the French Revolution. In J. C. Alexander (Ed.), *Durkheimian sociology: Cultural studies* (pp. 25-43). New York: Cambridge University Press.

Hunter, M. (1936). *Reaction to conquest.* Oxford: Oxford University Press.

Hutton, R. (1994). *The rise and fall of merry England: The ritual year, 1400-1700.* New York: Oxford University Press.

Huxley, J. (1966a). Introduction. *Philosophical transactions of the Royal Society of London, 251* (Series B, 772), 249-271.

Huxley, J. (Ed.). (1966b). A discussion of ritualization of behaviour in animals and man. *Philosophical transactions of the Royal Society of London, 251* (Series B, 772), 247-526.

Hymes, D. (1975). Breakthrough into performance. In D. Ben-Amos & K. S. Goldstein (Eds.), *Folklore: Performance and communication* (pp. 11-74). The Hague: Mouton.

Johnson, S., & Meinhof, U. H. (Eds.). (1997). *Language and masculinity.* Oxford: Blackwell.

Johnston, W. M. (1991). *Celebrations: The cult of anniversaries in Europe and the United States today.* New Brunswick: Transaction Press.

Kasson, J. F. (1990). *Rudeness & civility: Manners in nineteenth-century urban America.* New York: Hill & Wang.

Katz, E. (1980). Media events: The sense of occasion. *Studies in Visual Anthropology, 6,* 84-89.

Katz, E., & Dayan, D. (1986). Contests, conquests, coronations: On media events and their heroes. In C. F. Graumann & S. Moscovici (Eds.), *Changing conceptions of leadership* (pp. 135-144). New York: Springer-Verlag.

Katz, E., Blumler, J. G., & Gurevitch, M. (1974). Utilization of mass communication by the individual. In J. G. Blumler & E. Katz (Eds.), *The uses of mass communications: Current perspectives on gratifications research* (pp. 19-32). Beverly Hills, CA: Sage.

Kelly, J. D., & Kaplan, M. (1990). History, structure, and ritual. *Annual Review of Anthropology, 19,* 119-150.

Kertzer, D. I. (1988). *Ritual, politics, & power.* New Haven, CT: Yale University Press.

Kinkade, P. T., & Katovich, M. A. (1992). Toward a sociology of cult films: Reading *Rocky Horror. The Sociological Quarterly, 33,* 191-209.

Kirkwood, W. G. (1992). Narrative and the rhetoric of possibility. *Communication Monographs, 59,* 30-47.

Knuf, J. (1989-90). Where cultures meet: Ritual code and organizational boundary management. *Research on Language and Social Interaction, 23,* 109-138.

Knuf, J. (1993). "Ritual" in organizational culture theory: Some theoretical reflections and a plea for greater terminological rigor. *Communication Yearbook, 16,* 61-103.

Knuf, J. (1994). Ritual and irony: Observations about the discourse of political change in two Germanies. *Quarterly Journal of Speech, 80,* 174-194.

Kohák, E. V. (1966). Translator's introduction: The philosophy of Paul Ricoeur. In P. Ricoeur, *Freedom and Nature: The voluntary and the involuntary* (E. V. Kohák, Trans.) (pp. xi-xxxviii). Chicago: Northwestern University Press.

Koziol, G. (1992). *Begging pardon and favor: Ritual and political order in early medieval France.* Ithaca, NY: Cornell University Press.

Kramarae, C. (1981). *Women and men speaking.* Rowley, MA: Newbury House.

Kuipers, J. C. (1990). *Power in performance: The creation of textual authority in Weyewa ritual speech.* Philadelphia: University of Pennsylvania Press.

Lakoff, R. (1975). *Language and woman's place.* New York: Harper & Row.

Lane, C. (1981). *The rites of rulers: Ritual in industrial society—the Soviet case.* Cambridge: Cambridge University Press.

Lazarsfeld, P. (1940). *Radio and the printed page.* New York: Duell, Sloan & Pearce.

Lazarsfeld, P., & Merton, R. K. (1948). Mass communication, popular taste, and organized social action. In L. Bryson (Ed.), *The communication of ideas* (pp. 95-118). New York: Harper & Bros.

Leach, E. R. (1954). *Political systems of highland Burma: A study of Kachin social structure.* Cambridge, MA: Harvard University Press.

Leach, E. R. (1966). Ritualization in man in relation to conceptual and social development. *Philosophical transactions of the Royal Society of London, 251* (Series B, 772), 403-408.

Leach, E. R. (1968). Ritual. *International encyclopedia of the social sciences* (Vol. 13, pp. 520-526). New York: Macmillan.

Leach, E. R. (1976). *Culture and communication: The logic by which symbols are connected. An introduction to the use of structuralist analysis in social anthropology.* Cambridge: Cambridge University Press.

Leach, E. R. (1982). *Social anthropology.* New York: Oxford University Press.

Lemish, D. (1982). The rules of viewing television in public places. *Journal of Broadcasting, 26,* 757-782.

Lévi-Strauss, C. (1963). *Structural anthropology* (C. Jacobson & B. G. Schoepf, Trans.). New York: Basic Books. (Original work published 1958)

Lévi-Strauss, C. (1966). *The savage mind.* Chicago: University of Chicago Press. (Original work published 1962)

Lévi-Strauss, C. (1970). *The raw and the cooked: Introduction to a science of mythology,* Vol. 1 (J. Weightman & D. Weightman, Trans.). London: Jonathan Cape. (Original work published 1964)

Lewis, L. (Ed.). (1992). *Adoring audiences: Fan culture and popular media.* New York: Routledge.

Lincoln, B. (1989). *Discourse and the construction of society: Comparative studies of myth, ritual, and classification.* New York: Oxford University Press.

Lindlof, T. R., & Meyer, T. P. (1987). Mediated communication as ways of seeing, acting, and constructing culture: The tools and foundations of qualitative research. In T. R. Lindlof (Ed.), *Natural Audiences: Qualitative research of media uses and effects* (pp. 1-30). Norwood, NJ: Ablex.

Lorenz, K. (1970-71). *Studies in animal and human behavior,* (Vols. 1-2) (R. Martin, Trans.). Cambridge: Harvard University Press.

Lukes, S. (1972). *Emile Durkheim, his life and work: A historical and critical study.* New York: Harper & Row.

Lukes, S. (1975). Political ritual and social integration. *Sociology, 9,* 289-308.

Lull, J. (1980). The social uses of television. *Human Communication Research, 6,* 197-209.

Lull, J. (1982). A rules approach to the study of television and society. *Human Communication Research, 9,* 3-16.

Lutgendorf, P. (1990a). The power of sacred story: Ramayana recitation in contemporary North India. *Journal of Ritual Studies, 4,* 115-147.

Lutgendorf, P. (1990b). Ramayan: The video. *The Drama Review, 34,* 127-176.

Lutkehaus, N. C., & Roscoe, P. B. (1995). *Gender rituals: Female initiation in Melanesia.* New York: Routledge.

Lyons, A. P., & Lyons, H. D. (1987). Magical medicine on television: Benin City, Nigeria. *Journal of Ritual Studies, 1,* 103-136.

MacAloon, J. J. (1981). *This great symbol: Pierre de Coubertin and the origins of the Modern Olympic Games.* Chicago: University of Chicago Press.

MacAloon, J. J. (1982). Sociation and sociability in political celebrations. In V. Turner (Ed.), *Celebration: Studies in festivity and ritual* (pp. 255-271). Washington, DC: Smithsonian Institution Press.

MacAloon, J. J. (1984a). Olympic Games and the theory of spectacle in modern society. In J. J. MacAloon (Ed.), *Rite, drama, festival, spectacle: Rehearsals toward a theory of cultural performance* (pp. 241-280). Philadelphia: Institute for the Study of Human Issues.

MacAloon, J. J., (Ed.). (1984b). *Rite, drama, festival, spectacle: Rehearsals toward a theory of cultural performance.* Philadelphia: Institute for the Study of Human Issues.

MacAloon, J. J. (1989). Commentary: Critical data and rhetorical theory. *Critical Studies in Mass Communication, 6,* 183-194.

Malinowski, B. (1945). *Dynamics of cultural change.* New Haven, CT: Yale University Press.

Malinowski, B. (1948). *Magic, science and religion and other essays* (R. Redfield, Ed.). Glencoe, IL: Free Press.

Malinowski, B. (1949). Supplements I: The problem of meaning in primitive languages. In C. K. Ogden & I. A. Richards (Eds.), *The meaning of meaning: A study of the influence of language upon thought and of the science of symbolism* (10th ed.; pp. 296-336). New York: Harcourt Brace. (Original work published 1923)

Malinowski, B. (1953). *Argonauts of the western Pacific: An account of native enterprise and adventure in the archipelagoes of Melanesian New Guinea.* New York: Dutton. (Original work published 1922)

Manning, F. E. (Ed.). (1983). *The celebration of society: Perspectives on contemporary cultural performance.* Bowling Green, OH: Bowling Green University Popular Press.

Marsden, M. T. (1980). Television viewing as ritual. In R. B. Browne (Ed.), *Rituals and ceremonies in popular culture* (pp. 120-124). Bowling Green, OH: Bowling Green University Popular Press.

Marvin, C. (1994). Fresh blood, public meat: Rituals of totem regeneration in the 1992 presidential race. *Communication Research, 21,* 264-292.

McAdam, D. (1982). *Political process and the development of Black insurgency, 1930-1970.* Chicago: University of Chicago Press.

McGerr, M. E. (1986). *The decline of popular politics: The American north, 1865-1928.* New York: Oxford University Press.

McLeod, J. R. (1993). The ritual cycle of the American monarch. In P. R. Frese (Ed.), *Celebrations of identity: Multiple voices in American ritual performance* (pp. 195-222). Westport, CN: Bergin & Garvey.

Metcalf, P., & Huntington, R. (1991). *Celebrations of death: The anthropology of mortuary ritual* (2nd ed.). New York: Cambridge University Press.

Meyer, J. W., & Rowan, B. (1977). Institutionalized organizations: Formal structure as myth and ceremony. *American Journal of Sociology, 83,* 340-363.

Meyrowitz, J. (1985). *No sense of place: The impact of electronic media on social behavior.* New York: Oxford University Press.

Milic, L. T. (1987). Style, literary. *International Encyclopedia of Communications* (Vol. 4, pp. 185-188). New York: Oxford University Press.

Miller, D. (Ed.). (1993). *Unwrapping Christmas.* New York: Oxford University Press.

Modleski, T. (1983). The rhythms of reception: Daytime television and women's work. In E. A. Kaplan (Ed.), *Regarding television, critical approaches: An anthology* (pp. 67-75). Los Angeles: American Film Institute.

Moore, S. F., & Myerhoff, B. G. (Eds.). (1975). *Symbol and politics in communal ideology: Cases and questions.* Ithaca, NY: Cornell University Press.

Moore, S. F., & Myerhoff, B. G. (Eds.). (1977). *Secular ritual.* Assen, the Netherlands: Van Gorcum.

Myerhoff, B. G., Camino, L. A., & Turner, E. (1987). Rites of passage: An overview. *The encyclopedia of religion* (Vol. 12, pp. 380-386). New York: Macmillan.

Neurath, O. (1959). Sociology and physicalism (M. Magnus & R. Raico, Trans.). In A. J. Ayer (Ed.), *Logical positivism* (pp. 282-317). New York: Free Press. (Original work published 1931-32)

Neville, G. K. (1994). *The mother town: Civic ritual, symbol, and experience in the borders of Scotland.* New York: Oxford University Press.

Newcomb, H. M. (1978). Assessing the violence profile studies of Gerbner and Gross: A humanistic critique and suggestion. *Communication Research, 5,* 264-282.

Newcomb, H. M., & Hirsch, P. M. (1984). Television as a cultural forum: Implications for research. In W. D. Rowland, Jr., & B. Watkins (Eds.), *Interpreting television: Current research perspectives* (pp. 58-73). Beverly Hills, CA: Sage.

Ochs, D. J. (1993). *Consolatory rhetoric: Grief, symbol, and ritual in the Greco-Roman era.* Columbia: University of South Carolina Press.

Otnes, C., & Beltramini, R. F. (1996). *Gift giving: A research anthology.* Bowling Green, OH: Bowling Green State University Press.

Ozouf, M. (1988). *Festivals and the French revolution* (A. Sheridan, Trans.). Cambridge: Harvard University Press. (Original work published 1976)

Pacanowski, M. E., & O'Donnell-Trujillo, N. (1983). Organizational communication as cultural performance. *Communication Monographs, 50,* 126-147.

Paige, K. E., & Paige, J. M. (with Fuller, L., & Magnus, E.) (1981). *The politics of reproductive ritual.* Berkeley: University of California Press.

Parker, S. (1988). Rituals of gender: A study of etiquette, public symbols, and cognition. *American Anthropologist, 90,* 372-384.

Parsons, T. (1954). *Essays in sociological theory.* New York: Free Press. (Original work published 1944)

Parsons, T. (1964). *The social system.* New York: Free Press. (Original work published 1951)

Parsons, T. (1968). *The structure of social action* (Vols. 1-2). New York: Free Press. (Original work published 1937)

Parsons, T. (1969). On the concept of political power. In T. Parsons (Ed.), *Politics and social structure* (pp. 352-404). New York: Free Press.

Parsons, T., & Shils, E. A. (1951). Values, motives, and systems of action. In T. Parsons & E. A. Shils (Eds.), *Toward a general theory of action* (pp. 47-275). Cambridge, MA: Harvard University Press.

Payne, D. (1989). The Wizard of Oz: Therapeutic rhetoric in a contemporary media ritual. *Quarterly Journal of Speech, 75,* 25-39.

Peirce, C. S. (1932). *Collected papers of Charles Sanders Peirce, Volume II, Elements of logic* (C. Hartshorne & P. Weiss, Eds.). Cambridge: Harvard University Press.

Pencil, M. (1976). Salt passage research: The state of the art. *Journal of Communication, 26* (4), pp. 31-36.

Peters, J. D. (1986). Institutional sources of intellectual poverty in communication research. *Communication Research, 13,* 527-559.

Peters, J. D. (1990). Rhetoric's revival, positivism's persistence: Social science, clear communication, and the public space. *Sociological Theory, 2,* 224-231.

Peters, J. D. (1997, February). *Radio static and station identification as longing for the other.* Paper presented at Sound Research Seminar, University of Iowa, Iowa City, IA.

Peters, J. D., & Rothenbuhler, E. W. (1989). The reality of construction. In H. Simons (Ed.), *Perspectives on the rhetoric of the human sciences* (pp. 11-27). London: Sage.

Pfeffer, J. (1981). Management as symbolic action: The creation and maintenance of organizational paradigms. *Research in organizational behavior, 3,* 1-52.

Phillips, E. B. (1972). Approaches to objectivity: Journalistic and social science perspectives. In P. M. Hirsch, P. V. Miller, & F. G. Kline (Eds.), *Strategies for Communication Research* (pp. 63-77). Beverly Hills, CA: Sage.

Pickering, W. S. F. (1984). *Durkheim's sociology of religion: Themes and theories.* London: Routledge & Kegan Paul.

Powell, W. W., & DiMaggio, P. J. (Eds.). (1991). *The new institutionalism in organizational analysis.* Chicago: University of Chicago Press.

Radcliffe-Brown, A. R. (1922). *The Andaman islanders: A study in social anthropology.* Cambridge: Cambridge University Press.

Radcliffe-Brown, A. R. (1965). *Structure and function in primitive society: Essays and addresses.* Glencoe, IL: The Free Press. (Original work published 1952)

Rappaport, R. A. (1968). *Pigs for the ancestors: Ritual in the ecology of a New Guinea people.* New Haven, CT: Yale University Press.

Rappaport, R. A. (1979). *Ecology, meaning, & religion.* Berkeley: North Atlantic Books.

Rappaport, R. A. (1989). Ritual. *International encyclopedia of communications* (Vol. 3, pp. 467-473). New York: Oxford University Press.

Rawls, A. W. (1987). The interaction order *sui generis*: Goffman's contribution to social theory. *Sociological Theory, 5,* 136-149.

Reeves, J. L. (1988). Television stardom: A ritual of social typification and individualization. In J. W. Carey (Ed.), *Media, myths, and narratives: Television and the press* (pp. 146-160). Newbury Park, CA: Sage.

Reeves, E. B., & Bylund, R. A. (1989). Social density and public ritual in non-industrial communities: A cross-cultural analysis. *Sociological Quarterly, 30,* 225-244.

Reiss, D. (1981). *The family's construction of reality.* Cambridge, MA: Harvard University Press.

Renckstorf, K., McQuail, D., & Jankowski, N. (1996). *Media use as social action.* London: John Libbey.

Ricoeur, P. (1966). *Freedom and nature: The voluntary and the involuntary* (E. V. Kohák, Trans.). Chicago: Northwestern University Press. (Original work published 1950)

Ricoeur, P. (1970). *Freud and philosophy: An essay on interpretation* (D. Savage, Trans.). New Haven, CT: Yale University Press.

Ricoeur, P. (1974). *The conflict of interpretations: Essays in hermeneutics* (D. Ihde, Ed.). Evanston, IL: Northwestern University Press.

Ricoeur, P. (1976). *Interpretation theory: Discourse and the surplus of meaning.* Fort Worth, TX: Texas Christian University Press.

Ricoeur, P. (1981). *Hermeneutics and the human sciences: Essays on language, action, and interpretation* (J. B. Thompson, Ed. & Trans.). Cambridge: Cambridge University Press.

Riordan, J. (1987). Soviet muscular socialism: A Durkheimian analysis. *Sociology of Sport Journal, 4,* 376-393.

Rosen, R. (1986). Soap operas: Search for yesterday. In T. Gitlin (Ed.), *Watching television* (pp. 42-67). New York: Pantheon.

Rosenthal, C. J., & Marshall, V. W. (1988). Generational transmission of family ritual. *American Behavioral Scientist, 31,* 669-684.

Rothenbuhler, E. W. (1987). Neofunctionalism for Mass Communication Theory. *Mass Communication Review Yearbook, 6,* 67-85.

Rothenbuhler, E. W. (1988a). The liminal fight: Mass strikes as ritual and interpretation. In J. C. Alexander (Ed.), *Durkheimian sociology: Cultural studies* (pp. 66-89). New York: Cambridge University Press.

Rothenbuhler, E. W. (1988b). Live broadcasting, media events, telecommunication, and social form. In David R. Maines & Carl Couch (Eds.), *Information, communication, and social structure* (pp. 231-243). Springfield, IL: Charles C. Thomas.

Rothenbuhler, E. W. (1988c). The living room celebration of the Olympic Games. *Journal of Communication, 38* (3), 61-81.

Rothenbuhler, E. W. (1989). Values and symbols in public orientations to the Olympic media event. *Critical Studies in Mass Communication, 6,* 138-157.

Rothenbuhler, E. W. (1995). The social distribution of participation in the broadcast Olympic Games. *The Journal of International Communication, 2,* 66-79.

Rothenbuhler, E. W., & Peters, J. D. (1997). Defining phonography: An experiment in theory. *Musical Quarterly, 81,* 242-264

Rubin, A. M. (1984). Ritualized and instrumental television viewing. *Journal of Communication, 34*(3), 67-77.

Sáenz, M. (1992). Television viewing as a cultural practice. *Journal of Communication Inquiry, 16*(2), 37-51.

Sahlins, M. (1976). *Culture and practical reason.* Chicago: University of Chicago Press.

Sapir, E. (1949). Symbolism. In D. G. Mandelbaum (Ed.), *Selected writings of Edward Sapir in language, culture, and personality* (pp. 564-568). Berkeley: University of California Press. (Original work published 1934)

Saussure, F. de (1966). *Course in general linguistics* (C. Bally & A. Sechehaye, Ed., W. Baskin, Trans.). New York: McGraw-Hill. (Original work published 1915)

Schechner, R. (1987). Drama: Performance and ritual. *Encyclopedia of Religion* (Vol. 4, pp. 436-446). New York: Macmillan.

Schramm, W. (1965). Communication in crisis. In B. S. Greenberg & E. B. Parker (Eds.), *The Kennedy assassination and the American public* (pp. 1-25). Stanford, CA: Stanford University Press.

Schudson, M. (1984). *Advertising, the uneasy persuasion: Its dubious impact on American society.* New York: Basic Books.

Schudson, M. (1989). How culture works: Perspectives from media studies on the efficacy of symbols. *Theory and Society, 18,* 153-180.

Schudson, M. (1994). Voting rites: Why we need a new concept of citizenship. *The American Prospect, 19* (Fall), 59-68.

Schutz, A. (1967). *The phenomenology of the social world* (G. Walsh & F. Lehnert, Trans.). Chicago: Northwestern University Press. (Original work published 1932)

Schwartz, B., & Barsky, S. F. (1977). The home advantage. *Social Forces, 55,* 641-661.

Scott, J. C. (1990). *Domination and the arts of resistance: Hidden transcripts.* New Haven, CT: Yale University Press.

Searle, J. R. (1969). *Speech acts: An essay in the philosophy of language.* Cambridge, MA: Cambridge University Press.

Selberg, T. (1993). Television and ritualization of everyday life. *Journal of Popular Culture, 26*(4), 3-10.

Shannon, C. E., & Weaver, W. (1963). *The mathematical theory of communication.* Urbana: University of Illinois Press. (Original work published 1949)

Shepherd, G. J., & Rothenbuhler, E. W. (1991). A synthetic perspective on goals and discourse. In Karen Tracy (Ed.), *Understanding Face to Face Interaction: Issues linking goals and discourse* (pp. 189-203). Hillsdale, NJ: Lawrence Erlbaum Associates.

Shils, E. (1966). Ritual and crisis. *Philosophical transactions of the Royal Society of London, 251* (Series B, 772), 447-450.

Shils, E. (1975). *Center and periphery: Essays in macrosociology.* Chicago: University of Chicago Press.

Shils, E. (1980). The calling of sociology. In E. Shils, *The calling of sociology and other essays on the pursuit of learning* (pp. 3-92). Chicago: University of Chicago Press.

Shils, E., & Young, M. (1975). The meaning of the coronation. In E. Shils, *Center and periphery: Essays in macrosociology* (pp. 135-152). Chicago: University of Chicago Press. (Original work published 1956)

Sigman, S. J. (1991). Handling the discontinuous aspects of continuous social relationships: Toward research on the persistence of social forms. *Communication Theory, 1,* 106-127.

Silverstone, R. (1988). Television myth and culture. In J. W. Carey (Ed.), *Media, myths, and narratives: Television and the press* (pp. 20-47). Newbury Park, CA: Sage.

Slote, B. (Ed.). (1963). *Myth and symbol: Critical approaches and applications.* Lincoln: University of Nebraska Press.

Slowikowski, S. S. (1991). Burning desire: Nostalgia, ritual, and the sport-festival flame ceremony. *Sociology of Sport Journal, 8,* 239-257.

Smith, H. N. (1950). *Virgin land: The American West as symbol and myth.* Cambridge, MA: Harvard University Press.

Smith, P. (1991). Codes and conflict: Toward a theory of war as ritual. *Theory and Society, 20,* 103-138.

Smith, W. J. (1977). *The behavior of communicating: An ethological approach.* Cambridge, MA: Harvard University Press.

Smith, W. R. (1956). *The religion of the Semites.* New York: Meridian Library. (Original work published 1889)

St. Clair Harvey, L. (1990). Temporary insanity: Fun, games, and tranformational ritual in American music video. *Journal of Popular Culture, 24,* 39-64.

Stark, R., & Bainbridge, W. S. (1985). *The future of religion: Secularization, revival and cult formation.* Berkeley: University of California Press.

Stevens, J. D. (1985). Social utility of sensational news: Murder and divorce in the 1920's. *Journalism Quarterly, 62,* 53-58.

Strong, P. M. (1988). Minor courtesies and macro structures. In P. Drew & A. Wootton (Eds.), *Erving Goffman: Exploring the interaction order* (pp. 228-249). Cambridge: Polity Press.

Stull, D. D., Maynard-Moody, S., & Mitchell, J. (1988). The ritual of reorganization in a public bureaucracy. *Qualitative Sociology, 11,* 215-233.

Sutherland, J. C., & Siniawsky, S. J. (1982). The treatment and resolution of moral violations on soap operas. *Journal of Communication, 32* (2), 67-74.

Tambiah, S. J. (1968). The magical power of words. *Man, 3* (new series), 175-208.

Thomas, K. (1971). *Religion and the decline of magic.* New York: Charles Scribner's Sons.

Thompson, K. (1990). Secularization and sacralization. In J. C. Alexander & P. Sztompka (Eds.), *Rethinking progress: Movements, forces, and ideas at the end of the 20th century* (pp. 161-181). Boston: Unwin Hyman.

Tilly, C. (1978). *From mobilization to revolution.* Reading, MA: Addison-Wesley.

Tinbergen, N. (1972-73). *The animal in its world: Explorations of an ethologist, 1932-1972* (Vols 1-2). Cambridge: Harvard University Press.

Tiryakian, E. A. (1988). From Durkheim to Managua: Revolutions as religious revivals. In J. C. Alexander (Ed.), *Durkheimian sociology: Cultural studies* (pp. 44-65). New York: Cambridge University Press.

Trent, J. S. (1978). Presidential surfacing: The ritualistic and crucial first act. *Communication Monographs, 45,* 281-292.

Trevor-Roper, H. (1983). The invention of tradition: The highland tradition of Scotland. In E. Hobsbawm & T. Ranger (Eds.), *The invention of tradition* (pp. 15-41). New York: Cambridge University Press.

Trotsky, L. (1960). *Literature and revolution.* Ann Arbor: University of Michigan Press. (Original work published 1924)

Trotsky, L. (1973). *Problems of everyday life; and other writings on culture & science.* New York: Monad Press.

Tuchman, G. (1972). Objectivity as strategic ritual. *American Journal of Sociology, 77,* 660-679.

Tuchman, G. (1978). *Making news: A study in the construction of reality.* New York: Free Press.

Turkle, S. R. (1975). Symbol and festival in the French student uprising (May - June 1968). In S. F. Moore & B. G. Myerhoff (Eds.), *Symbol and politics in communal ideology: Cases and questions* (pp. 68-100). Ithaca, NY: Cornell University Press.

Turner, V. (1957). *Schism and continuity in an African society: A study of Ndembu village life.* Manchester: Manchester University Press.

Turner, V. (1967). *The forest of symbols: Aspects of Ndembu ritual.* Ithaca, NY: Cornell University Press.

Turner, V. (1975). *Revelation and divination in Ndembu ritual.* Ithaca, NY: Cornell University Press.

Turner, V. (1977). *The ritual process: Structure and anti-structure.* Ithaca, NY: Cornell University Press. (Original work published 1969)

Turner, V. (1978). Encounter with Freud: The making of a comparative symbologist. In G. D. Spindler (Ed.), *The making of psychological anthropology* (pp. 559-583). Berkeley: University of California Press.

Turner, V. (Ed.). (1982a). *Celebration: Studies in festivity and ritual.* Washington, DC: Smithsonian Institution.

Turner, V. (1982b). *From ritual to theatre: The human seriousness of play.* New York: Performing Arts Journal Publications.

Tylor, E. B. (1924). *Primitive culture: Researches into the development of mythology, philosophy, religion, language, art, and custom* (7th ed., Vols. 1-2). New York: Brentano's. (Original work published 1871)

van Bremen, J. (1995). Introduction: The myth of the secularization of industrialized societies. In J. van Bremen & D. P. Martinez (Eds.), *Ceremony and ritual in Japan: Religious practices in an industrialized society* (pp. 1-22). New York: Routledge.

van Bremen, J., & Martinez, D. P. (Eds.). (1995). *Ceremony and ritual in Japan: Religious practices in an industrialized society.* New York: Routledge.

Vande Berg, L. R. (1995). Living room pilgrimages: Television's cyclical commemoration of the assassination anniversary of John F. Kennedy. *Communication Monographs, 62,* 47-64.

Wagner-Pacifici, R. E. (1986). *The Moro morality play: Terrorism as social drama.* Chicago: University of Chicago Press.

Wallace, A. F. C. (1966). *Religion: An anthropological view.* New York: Random House.

Warner, W. L. (1959). *Yankee city series, Vol. 5. The living and the dead: A study of the symbolic life of Americans.* New Haven: Yale University Press.

Watzlawick, P., Beavin, J. H., & Jackson, D. D. (1967). *Pragmatics of human communication: A study of interactional patterns, pathologies, and paradoxes.* New York: Norton.

Weber, M. (1978). *Economy and society* (G. Roth & C. Wittich, Eds.). Berkeley: University of California Press. (Original work published 1922)

Wenner, L. A., & Gantz, W. (1989). The audience experience with sports on television. In L. A. Wenner (Ed.), *Media, sports, and society* (pp. 241-269). Newbury Park, CA: Sage.

Wilentz, S. (Ed.). (1985). *Rites of power: Symbolism, ritual & politics since the Middle Ages.* Philadelphia: University of Pennsylvania Press.

Williams, R. (1974). *Television: Technology and cultural form.* New York: Schocken.

Williams, R. (1980). Advertising: The magic system. In R. Williams, *Problems in materialism and culture* (pp. 170-195). London: New Left Books.

Willis, P. E. (1978). *Profane culture.* London: Routledge & Kegan Paul.

Wilson, B. R. (1987). Secularization. *Encyclopedia of religion* (Vol. 13, pp. 159-165). New York: Macmillan.

Wilson, B. R. (1990). *The social dimensions of sectarianism: Sects and new religious movements in contemporary society.* Oxford: Clarendon.

Wilson, G., & Wilson, M. (1945). *Analysis of social change.* Cambridge: Cambridge University Press.

Wilson, M. (1972). The wedding cakes: A study of ritual change. In J. S. La Fontaine (Ed.), *The interpretation of ritual: Essays in honour of A. I. Richards* (pp. 187-201). London: Tavistock Publications.

Wolf, E. R. (1982). *Europe and the people without history.* Berkeley: University of California Press.

Wolin, S. J., & Bennett, L. A. (1984). Family rituals. *Family Process, 23,* 401-420.

Wolin, S. J., Bennett, L. A., Noonan, D. L., & Teitelbaum, M. A. (1980). Disrupted family rituals: A factor in the intergenerational transmission of alcoholism. *Journal of Studies on Alcohol, 41,* 199-214.

Wuthnow, R. J. (1988). Sociology of religion. In N. J. Smelser (Ed.), *Handbook of sociology* (pp. 473-509). Newbury Park, CA: Sage.

Young-Laughlin, J., & Laughlin, C. D. (1988). How masks work, or masks work how? *Journal of Ritual Studies, 2,* 59-86.

Zei, V. (1995). *Symbolic spaces of the nation-state: The case of Slovenia.* Unpublished doctoral dissertation, University of Iowa, Iowa City, IA.

Zelizer, B. (1990). Achieving journalistic authority through narrative. *Critical Studies in Mass Communication, 7,* 366-376.

Zelizer, B. (1992). *Covering the body: The Kennedy assassination, the media, and the shaping of collective memory.* Chicago: University of Chicago Press.

Zerubavel, Y. (1995). *Recovered roots: Collective memory and the making of Israeli national identity.* Chicago: University of Chicago Press.

Zucker, L. G. (1977). The role of institutionalization in cultural persistence. *American Sociological Review, 42,* 726-743.

Zuesse, E. M. (1987). Ritual. *Encyclopedia of religion* (Vol. 12, pp. 405-422). New York: Macmillan.

Author Index

Subject Index

About the Author

Eric W. Rothenbuhler is Associate Professor of Communication Studies at the University of Iowa, where he has been teaching since earning his doctorate at the Annenberg School of Communications at the University of Southern California in 1985. His teaching and research address the variety of ways in which communication participates in the integration of individual and social orders, including communication and community, communication rituals, and media industries as producers of popular culture.